MW00675643

JOY
comes
in the
MORNING

Also by Don Anderson

Abraham: Delay Is Not Denial
Ecclesiastes: The Mid-Life Crisis
Song of Solomon: Make Full My Joy
A Gift Too Wonderful for Words
Joseph: Fruitful in Affliction
God Wants a Relationship Not a Performance

Don Anderson

JOY comes in the MORNING

The Glorious Victory of the Resurrection

LOIZEAUX BROTHERS
Neptune, New Jersey

Printed in the United States of America.

A publication of Loizeaux Brothers, Inc.
A nonprofit organization devoted to the Lord's work and to the spread of his truth.

New Testament scripture quotations, not otherwise noted, are taken from the author's personal translation of the Greek text.

Library of Congress Cataloging-in-Publication Data
Anderson, Don, 1933-
Joy Comes in the Morning/Don Anderson.
p. cm.
Includes bibliographical references.
ISBN 0-87213-006-1
1. Easter. 2. Jesus Christ—Resurrection. I. Title.
BV55.A53 1990 89-35935
232'.5—dc20 CIP

The author wishes to acknowledge the editorial assistance of Jane Rodgers.

D E D I C A T I O N

Jane Rodgers

Without Jesus there would be no Easter, and without Jane there would be no book. Her name means "gift of God," and she has been just that to Pearl and me. Her long hours of tireless organizing, outlining, and rewriting these pages have made it all possible.

Special Thanks

Any book is the product of numerous folks to whom I'm deeply indebted. With much gratitude, I'd like to acknowledge the following ones.

Peter Bartlett and Claudia Mooij from Loizeaux Brothers, for believing in us and being so supportive. What joy it is to work with them.

The members of the Ministries staff: Mark and Donna, Carter and Georgia, Paul and Harriet, Jan, Jean, Linda, Sandra, Julea. Fellow soldiers, every one.

From our Ministries board: Chairman Bill and Dorothy Lawrence, Dick and Virginia Allen, Jerry and Leta Arrington, Lee and Nancy Bailey, Bill and Judy Dunn, Kirk and Susan Hays, Asa and Billie Holleman, David and Nona Jackson, Dick and Ethel Knarr, Bill and Peggy Kyser, Terry and Laurie Ledbetter, Rusty and Donna Leftwich, Al and Darlene McNatt, John and Loretta Miller, Tom and Jean Paulk, Mike and Jane Rodgers, Mike and Myrna Schoenfeld, David and Melina Shellenberger, Mark and Donna Skorheim, Jerry and Gail Smith, Martine and Peggy Tirmenstein, Randy and Carol Wolff; and Pat Guion, who encourages us all, even as we, with her, miss Don.

From the board at Hide-A-Way Lake Community Church: Chairman Tom and Wink Sheffield, Merritt and Anne Barker, Bob and Ollie Borchardt, Emery and Janet Crane, Jim and Jean Duncan, Al and Sara Dunn, Barham and Linda Fulmer, Charlie and Marie Haas, Zeke and Boots Langdon, Tom and Jean Paulk, Bob and Ruth Sielken, Howard and June Sinclair, Jim and Barbara Wilson.

From the board at Emerald Bay Community Church: Chairman Wilbur and Margie Woods, Betty Dettre, Bill and Kay Kutner, Tom and Joyce Madden, Al and Linda Nauck, Duane and Betty Puckett, Mike and Janet Vereeke.

Pearl, my wife of thirty-five years, who has given birth to our tribe of five and stood with me to laugh and to cry. Faithful and consistent, she is always there with words of affirmation and encouragement.

And last but not least, the Fabulous Five: Donna, Rebecca, Robert, Grant, and Julea. You are loved by your daddy.

אֲנִי לְדוֹדִי וְדוֹדִי לִי

I am my beloved's, and my beloved is mine
Song of Solomon 6:3

πάυτα χαὶ έυ πᾶσιυ Χφιστόζ

Christ is all, and in all
Colossians 3:11

CONTENTS

Foreword 11

PART ONE
The Long Night

1. The Long Night . . . the Joyous Morning 15
2. Behold, Your King 21
   Matthew 21:1-11
3. The Suffering Servant 45
   Isaiah 52:13–53:12
4. The Psalm of the Cross 75
   Psalm 22

PART TWO
The Joyous Morning

5. The Record of the Resurrection 115
   Mark 16:1-8
6. Responses to the Resurrection 137
   John 20:1-31
7. To Emmaus and Back 165
   Luke 24:13-36
8. The Great Cover-Up 195
   Matthew 28:11-20
9. The Resurrection 221

Bibliography and Suggested Readings 243
Acknowledgments 246

F O R E W O R D

Satan always fogs in the area of the crucial. Like acid rain, he eats away at redemptive history and turns its momentous occasions into worldly celebration. Is it any wonder he has robbed the manger and the tomb of their critical significance? People in our world march on to a christless eternity because they have not bowed themselves before the mysteries of Bethlehem, Calvary, and the shattered tomb.

The resurrection of Christ is the fundamental event of human history. Yet one searches in vain in this world's supermarket for any clue as to what his being raised from the dead is all about. If such information exists, it is buried under Easter eggs, bunny rabbits, and baby chicks. Easter, for many people, has become a pilgrimage to an annual ecclesiastical open house. Perhaps the United States is rapidly becoming the largest spiritual nursery in the world, because it has neglected the cosmic implications of Jesus Christ. Theology begins and ends with that one great fact.

When all else fails, read the directions.

Joy Comes in the Morning by Don Anderson brings us back to the life-changing truths of the death and resurrection of our Lord Jesus Christ. With wit, insight, and expertise, Don invites us to join him on a pilgrimage through sections of the Old Testament and the gospels that climaxes in a discussion of the ramifications of the resurrection. Old truths are "resurrected," new truths are discovered, as this skilled communicator invites us to consider anew the wonder of the resurrection. As we take a tour through the historical documents, we are sharply reminded of their continuity and central theme: Jesus Christ.

Biblical characters and locations come to life as we view

Jesus' humble entrance into the city of Jerusalem on Palm Sunday. Tears well up in us as the realities of death by crucifixion are vividly brought to mind. The prophet Isaiah and the psalmist remind us of the suffering servant and his role as the sin bearer.

Joy wells in our hearts as we hear the divine orchestra play the "Hallelujah Chorus." We see the lightning break through darkness, the shattered stone, empty grave clothes. Deftly the author brings us from the events of the resurrection to our celebration of it. He closes with practical suggestions for keeping Christ central this Easter and for igniting our hearts to burn for him. May God use this book to accomplish those noble objectives.

JOSEPH C. ALDRICH
President, Multnomah School of the Bible

PART ONE

The Long Night

C H A P T E R O N E

The Long Night . . . The Joyous Morning

Easter. What is it to you? To the world, Easter is what Christmas used to be. Think about it a moment, and you'll know what I mean.

Do you remember when Christmas decorations didn't deck the stores until the day after Thanksgiving? I do. Nowadays we're hard pressed to hit Halloween without walking under plastic mistletoe, bumping up against synthetic holly, and tripping over strings of blinking lights. Actually, I'm told, one can notice small signs of Christmas cheer as soon as the back-to-school sales end in September.

I'm resigned to this early yuletide blitz. I can deal with Santa in September and plastic poinsettias in early fall. I've reluctantly accepted the fact that the world's celebration of our savior's birth is by and large a secularized scene. After all, it was way back in the Middle Ages that Christmas celebrations became so rowdy that the Puritans in England later did away by law with observance of the holiday. We shouldn't be surprised when, in the world's eye, the sacred birth shares the stage with a jolly old jelly-bellied elf.

Don't get me wrong. I'm not advocating that we approve of

overcommercialized Christmases. As Christians we should be saddened at the supersecularization of Jesus' birth. Our hearts should ache as the message of the coming of the savior is obscured underneath rolls of wrapping paper, yards of ribbon, piles of packages, weeks of parties, and mountains of bills. It is important that our children remember holiday traditions—special ornaments, stuffed stockings, Christmas dinners, family gatherings—but it is also crucial that the reason for the season never be forgotten.

Let's admit it. In a society where merchants start planning for next year's Christmas push immediately after January inventories, the overcommercialization of the holiday is a given. We can stress the sacred in our own homes and churches, and we can determine beforehand not to embark on buying binges ad nauseam, but we'll never be able to do much about curbing the commercialism of Christmas. We live in an indulge-till-you-bulge culture, and as long as that's true, Christmas will be the premiere occasion for parties, presents, deferred payments, and near pandemonium. The plain truth is, come January, many of our friends will be wishing they could disappear—in hopes that American Express, Visa, and MasterCard won't know where to find them.

What bothers me is not Christmas. What concerns me is that Easter seems to be following suit.

The dying glow of yuletide lights signals the subtle start of the season for cellophane grass, stuffed bunnies, chocolate eggs, and straw baskets. Oh, there's Valentine's Day to contend with first, but quite soon the same photographers who snapped photos of our kids on Santa's lap have told Santa to slip on a fuzzy pink rabbit suit and sit down for more pictures. How well they know what parents are willing to shell out for those shots with the Easter bunny. Soon after the new year, catalogs featuring bunny gifts, crystal eggs, and springtime specials start arriving in the mailbox. By mid-February, the stores are stocked with spring clothes and the push is on for Easter outfits. Once emptied of their Valentine's Day stock, card stores fill the racks with Easter sentiments. Boxed Easter cards are now available, like those we can buy at Christmas time.

Things used to be different, and it wasn't so long ago. Before unaccustomed affluence enveloped our society in the '60s, '70s, and '80s, Easters were simpler times. There were no Easter gifts. Perhaps you bought Bibles for the children one year. Of course egg hunts, chocolate bunnies (solid, please!), new clothes, and family dinners were standard Easter fare. Going to church on Easter Sunday was expected too. Even the unchurched felt the need for some spiritual exercise; besides, the music was always so pretty. Gradually we've moved away from such simplicity.

Things aren't out of hand—yet.

But then, Christmas wasn't *always* a mass of commercialism either.

I move that as Christians we do what we can to discourage the development of Easter extravaganzas. Do I hear a second?

Just as it's crucial for us to recall that Christ is the crux of the Christmas season, let's determine never to forget why we buy lilies and sing special music at Easter. At the last supper, as he broke bread and offered it to his disciples, Jesus said, "This do in remembrance of me" (Luke 22:19 KJV). The instruction is *to remember.* We cannot allow the truth of a crucified and risen savior to become obscured underneath mounds of cellophane grass, colored eggs, china rabbits, dyed chicks, and barely opened Bibles.

The Real Reason

When reminiscing about the Easters of her childhood on the family farm in Oklahoma, my wife Pearl recalls that Easter Sunday was special. It was the day when long underwear was finally put away. Woolen stockings were rolled up and heavy shoes stored, to be replaced by cotton anklets and, best of all, shiny new patent leather shoes for church. Out came new dresses and matching bonnets, specially made for the occasion. Colored eggs were hidden, to the delight of the kids. Cholesterol levels weren't an issue then, so breakfast consisted of eggs—stuffed or boiled or scrambled or fried. It was a special time, a rite of passage into spring, the day after which the children started clamoring for permission to go barefoot, with reasonable hopes of receiving a yes.

Despite the springtime sentiments, Pearl also recalls that she and her brothers and sisters understood why Easter was important. They enjoyed the eggs and Easter clothes, but the sideshow never got in the way of the main event. "The way we celebrated," she reflects, "did not take away from the resurrection." Pearl goes on, "I think each of our own five kids would say the same thing. When asked about the importance of Easter, they'd answer, 'The resurrection,' and memories of fun and games and Easter baskets would be secondary." I agree with her.

My chief reason for writing this book is that I fear we Christians are in danger of distancing ourselves from the heart-wrenching reality of the cross and the glory of its aftermath. We're in danger of letting the fun and games replace the resurrection in significance. We're becoming caught up in the commercial shuffle of Easter, when more than anything else Easter should be a time in which we stand in awe of a savior who cared enough to come and to die, a savior whom death could not contain.

Easter is the sequel to Christmas; it's the rest of the story. One is the beginning and the other the end of the incarnation. We're going to take a look at the cross, and we're going to meet the men and women who either stood at its foot, or else fled for high ground. May we never become cold and complacent about the intensity of the Lord's torment or the misery of his separation from the Father. After we look at the cross, we'll focus our attention on the resurrection, the hallelujah chorus in the drama of redemption. Without his arising, Jesus' death would have been meaningless—just another dismal end to another religious fanatic, another sacrifice, another martyr who found a cause to die for, who bit off more than he could chew in tackling the powers that be. Nothing all that unusual.

When deciding on the title of this book, after much thought and prayer Psalm 30 came to mind. It's a song of thanksgiving, a shout of joy. Its superscription reads: "A Song at the Dedication of the House" (NASB). The title may refer to David's dedication of the site of the temple that would eventually be built by his son Solomon. We can tell from reading the text that David had suffered much physically and/or emotionally. Many commentators think that the psalm was written as a result of David's intense guilt at having disobeyed God by pridefully ordering a census taken of the Israelites. God's response to his disobedience was to permit a plague to infect the land, and some seventy thousand of David's subjects perished. Perhaps too, David had figured he'd fall victim to the ravaging disease. Certainly he felt tremendous remorse for having brought such judgment on his people. Whatever David's circumstances, he had evidently seen the hand of the Lord in delivering him and the nation, and his psalm is a song of joy and gratitude at God's great mercy. The night may be long, God's discipline may fall fiercely, but joy comes in the morning. The Lord's anger is transitory; his love and favor last forever.

Let's look at the first five verses of Psalm 30:

> I will extol Thee, O Lord, for
> Thou hast lifted me up,
> And hast not let my enemies
> rejoice over me.
> O Lord my God,
> I cried to Thee for help, and
> Thou didst heal me.
> O Lord, Thou hast brought up
> my soul from Sheol;
> Thou hast kept me alive, that I
> should not go down to the
> pit.

Sing praise to the Lord, you
His godly ones,
And give thanks to His holy
name.
For His anger is but for a moment,
His favor is for a lifetime:
Weeping may last for the night,
But a shout of joy comes in the
morning (Psalm 30:1-5 NASB).

Look at that message. God's "anger is but for a moment, His favor is for a lifetime. Weeping may last for the night, But a shout of joy comes in the morning." David's private crisis and deliverance from the crunch are chronicled there, yet on reading it, one cannot help but notice the messianic overtones. How sharply the words remind us of what happened when Jesus mounted a knoll outside Jerusalem and allowed himself to be nailed to the cross, there to die, and then to rise again on the third day.

The night? For humankind, it came in the garden of Eden, where human rebellion resulted in broken relationship with the creator. The night was long, covering thousands of years and full of weeping, becoming the blackest at a three-hour point of time on which all history pivots—the three hours in which Jesus Christ was miraculously made sin for us in the sight of the Father.

As the Lord's limp body was slowly lowered from the beams, wrapped in linen grave clothes, and placed inside a sealed tomb, the night continued.

Then the rosy hues of Easter dawn moved above the horizon to reveal an empty tomb and discarded shroud, watched over by angels who proclaimed, "HE IS RISEN!"

Thus the long night ended.

Joy comes in the morning.

C H A P T E R T W O

Behold, Your King

Matthew 21:1-11

Picture the scene in your mind. It was spring break from Torah University, and Levi, Reuben, and Joshua headed south for some days of fun in the sun on the Red Sea. They returned to Jerusalem late Friday afternoon, in anticipation of the sabbath. Classes were to resume on Monday for a short week before Passover, so there would be a day or so to kill in the big city.

Something was different about Jerusalem that Friday. Reuben noticed it first. There was an undeniable undercurrent of tension. Tempers ran high. People were on edge. Groups of young men like themselves roamed the streets, looking for something to stir up—rebels in search of a cause. Talk about this Jesus person seemed everywhere. Women whispered about him in the marketplace. Men debated about him in the synagogues and public meeting places; they spoke about how they would like to rid themselves of the insulting yoke of Roman oppression. Was he the promised messiah? Could he be the one sent from God to lead them in a revolution against the government?

This Jesus of Nazareth was powerful—that was for sure. People said he had even raised a man from the dead. A fellow named Lazarus it was; the man lived nearby in the town of

Bethany. Jesus had also healed the lepers, the lame, and the blind, people said. He was outspoken too, openly critical of the Pharisees and religious leaders. Maybe he *was* a modern-day Moses, come to set his people free.

Levi, Reuben, and Joshua sat in on every conversation they found where the topic was Jesus. He'd been brought up at school, but the professors had stifled the discussions. Even mentioning Isaiah 53 landed one student in hot water last semester; the rabbi had turned purple and stalked out of the room. The three young men in Jerusalem wanted to know more, and now it appeared they'd get their chance. The rumor was that this Nazarene was on his way here, bringing crowds with him up from Jericho. Messengers had gotten wind of his approach and delivered that news, along with the mail. His estimated time of arrival wasn't until after the sabbath, maybe as early as Sunday morning. Whenever he came, Levi, Reuben, and Joshua knew they'd be around for his arrival. Smack in the midst of the tension-packed city was exactly where they wanted to be, right in the big middle of this Jesus thing, whatever it was. Like student protesters from Czechoslovakia to Beijing, they longed to be in the thick of it.

Does that sound far-fetched to you? The situation described above wasn't unlikely at all. Young Jewish males of Jesus' day did receive strict instruction from the rabbis, but there were holidays. Very probably a trio of young adults like these three found themselves footloose and curious within the walls of the teeming city of Jerusalem on a Friday afternoon, the start of a weekend the world would never forget.

It wouldn't be Jesus' first journey to the city of his human destiny. He'd been to Jerusalem often before. But this time was special. Actually, *special* is hardly the word. Try *significant beyond measure*, a time that would impact the entire human race, even the entire universe with its consequences. Christ's entrance into Jerusalem on what we call Palm Sunday was the presentation of a king to his people, the complete, literal fulfillment of what had been prophesied centuries before, a flesh and blood enactment of the age-old promises of God to his children. And somehow, most of the Levis, Reubens, and Joshuas missed it.

As we'll see, on that Sunday, the Christ didn't come as the people of Israel expected. Oh, they greeted him royally, to be sure, but before a week passed, they rejected his humility-cloaked majesty, and he was hanging from a cross. For the throngs in Jerusalem, the countdown to his crucifixion started on the Sunday he entered the city. The reality is that the wheels had been set in motion long before that, soon after the creation of humankind, in fact.

We're going to look closely at Matthew's account of Jesus' entrance into the busy, bustling city of Jerusalem. We'll meet the people; we'll soak in the sights and surroundings. But before we find ourselves eyewitnesses to that Palm Sunday, let's briefly look within scripture and discover that every tragedy and triumph of Easter week was part of God's plan for us.

Tracing the Seed

Who was this Jesus who mounted the foal of a donkey and rode into Jerusalem, cheered by masses of men, women, and children spreading garments and greenery before him and shouting with joy at his coming? Who was this Jesus who later in the week bowed his bloodied head and gave up his spirit, three days afterward to shatter the shackles of physical death and arise from the grave?

Who was Jesus? Or better, who *is* Jesus? He is God almighty, one third of what we call the trinity: God the Son, God the Father, God the Spirit. As God the Son, Jesus Christ coexists eternally with the Father and the Spirit (Genesis 1:26; John 8:58). He was present at the creation of the world (John 1:1-2; Colossians 1:16-17). Like the magi coming from the east after his birth, who spontaneously bowed before him, we Christians respond to him in worship. Of him we can legitimately cry, "Hail, the heaven-born prince of peace! Hail, the incarnate deity!" Jesus came to earth as God incarnate, God clothed in human flesh. On earth he was wholly human and wholly divine, living the perfect life that only God could accomplish and dying as a spotless sacrifice to pay the penalty for the sins of humanity and to open a gateway to glory for all who believe in his name (John 1:29; 3:16).

The first time Christ is directly mentioned in scripture is in Genesis 3:15. You know the story. Conned by Satan, and victims of their own desire, Adam and Eve snatched bites of the fruit of the one tree forbidden them in the paradise God had created for them. Instantaneously their eyes opened to the realities of good and evil. The uninhibited fellowship with him which God had intended for them to share was destroyed by their willful disobedience. They were ousted from the lush garden and condemned to suffer the agonies of human existence, including physical death. But there was hope.

From the fearfulness of judgment came the voice of God with a promise of restored fellowship, a promise of one who would come to rebuild the bridge of broken relationship, a messiah who would be savior to the helpless and hopeless. Jesus was that promised seed. This offspring of the woman (Genesis 3:15) was none other than God the Son, who centuries later allowed himself to be born of a virgin. Although his conception was the supernatural work of the Holy Spirit, his birth was quite ordinary, awash in blood and tears like that of any human child (see Luke 2:6-7).

During his thirty-three years on earth, he experienced temptation, but never succumbed to it. He knew hunger, thirst, weariness, and homelessness. He healed the infirm, cast out demons, and resurrected the dead. Winds and tides obeyed him. He embraced sinners and scorned the self-righteous. He blasted hypocritical religious leaders and incurred their wrath with his honesty. He claimed to be the water of life, slaking the thirst of sinful humanity; the bread of life, satisfying the hungry heart; the light of the world, shining with transparent truth.

He solved the mystery of death by purporting to be the resurrection and the life. He maintained that he was the door, the shepherd, the way, the truth, the life. He claimed to be one with the Father. He was executed because the people he had chosen for singular honor would neither accept him nor acknowledge his right to rule. Even in his death there was enormous victory because the grave could not contain him. His resurrection broke the grip of Satan on the human race for all time by enabling any who will come to him in faith to experience forgiveness and a permanent relationship with him.

In the book of Genesis we again hear of Jesus, this promised seed, when God spoke to an unknown sheepmaster from an obscure town called Ur of the Chaldees. To this man, Abram (later to be known as Abraham), God obligated himself unconditionally in what we know as the abrahamic covenant. In Genesis 12:1-3, the Lord commanded Abraham to fold up his tents, round up his livestock, say goodbye to his relatives, and quietly steal away from his homeland for a destination known only to God. As God revealed, this mysterious land, which we know as Canaan or modern-day Israel and Palestine, would belong to Abraham and his descendants, who would become a "great nation."

It all sounds plausible enough, until you realize that at the moment God called him forth from Ur, Abraham was seventy-five years old and childless. Besides, he was married to a sixty-five-year-old woman, Sarah, who happened to be barren. Ideas of babies and diapers had long since fallen by the wayside for this geriatric pair. Then Abraham heard the voice of God.

In his sovereign purpose, and in his time, God blessed Abraham and Sarah with a baby boy, Isaac. When, nearly a quarter century after calling Abraham out of Ur, God announced that Isaac would be born within a year, he also miraculously sealed his unconditional covenant with Abraham, stating for the first time that his promises of a land and a seed were everlasting. God obligated himself to fulfill his word to Abraham unconditionally, with no strings attached (Genesis 17:7-8). All Abraham had to do was accept God's offer by faith. Because of what God would do, not because of what Abraham had done or could do on his own, Abraham's descendants would become a great nation called the Jews or Hebrews. They would eternally possess a promised land, and would produce, eventually, an eternal seed, an eternal heir.

From Abraham to his son Isaac to Isaac's son Jacob, the line of the promised seed continued. Jacob's twelve sons became the patriarchs of the twelve tribes of the nation of Israel. Through Jacob's fourth-born son, Judah, a child of Jacob's marriage to Leah, the line of the promised eternal seed continued. An elderly, ailing Jacob lay on his death bed and imparted his final words of blessing and promise to the sons who had gathered around him. In this scene of farewell the dying father described Judah's descendants as a kingly tribe, saying:

> The scepter shall not depart from Judah,
> Nor the ruler's staff from between his feet,
> Until Shiloh comes,
> And to him shall be the obedience of the peoples
> (Genesis 49:10 NASB).

In God's plan for the emerging nation of Israel, Judah's family was to be the royal line. Kings and princes and rulers would descend from him. The greatest of these was to be Shiloh. The term refers to Jesus Christ, the messiah, the savior, the promised seed who numbers among Judah's descendants (see also Numbers 24:17). The Hebrew word for Shiloh means "place of rest" or "tranquility." No wonder Jesus later issued this invitation: "Come to Me, all who are weary and heavy laden, and I will give you rest" (Matthew 28:28 NASB; see also 28:29-30).

Before Christ's human birth centuries later, another of Judah's descendants, David, king of Israel, received a special communication from God through the prophet Nathan. It is known to us as the davidic covenant, and at its close, the Lord revealed something amazing to David: "Your house and your kingdom will endure forever before me; your throne will be established forever" (2 Samuel 7:16 NIV). God didn't promise that David would live forever, but that his throne would exist forever and that one of his descendants would reign eternally. If we are to believe God, then a special king, a descendant of David, will sit on an everlasting throne. This heir can be none other than Jesus Christ, the God-man, known also as the Son of David because both of his earthly parents, Mary and Joseph, were descendants of David and members of the tribe of Judah (see Luke 2:4-5).

According to God's word, an eternal throne, an everlasting kingdom, will be Christ's. The complete fulfillment of this prophecy remains to be seen. Yet the prophetic clock revealed in the biblical books of Jeremiah, Daniel, Ezekiel, Zechariah, and the Revelation is steadily ticking down. We can count on it that someday, perhaps very soon, the trumpet will sound and the Lord will call for his own. He'll descend with a shout and snatch away his bride, the church, sparing Christians from a holocaust that will follow. Paul described this prophetic event, known as the rapture of the church, in 1 Thessalonians 4:16-18:

> For the Lord Himself will descend from heaven with a shout, with the voice of the archangel, and with the trumpet of God; and the dead in Christ shall rise first. Then we who are alive and remain shall be caught up together with them in the clouds to meet the Lord in the air, and thus we shall always be with the Lord (NASB).

Paul also tells us in 1 Corinthians 15:51-52 that this reunion with our Lord will take place instantly, in the twinkling of an eye. First those believers who have died, then those of us who remain, will receive glorious new immortal bodies, and up we'll go. Believe me, you'll want to be along for the ride. We'll be spared the horror of the period of famine and war called the tribulation—seven years of catastrophic chaos, dictatorial deception, satanic slaughter of the saints. Acts of God in nature will rain judgment as the stars fall; the earth will quake; hundred-pound hailstones will pummel the terrain; the sun will scorch; and the seas, rivers, and springs will become blood.

After the tribulation period, heaven will open and Jesus will come as king of kings and Lord of lords. (Revelation 19:11-16). His feet will touch the mount of Olives, splitting it asunder. A word from his mouth will forever silence the kings of the world arrayed to oppose him in the battle of Armageddon (see Revelation 19:17-21). All the nations of the earth will come from north, south, east, and west to destroy Abraham's seed. But Jesus Christ will secure a total victory over the nations of the earth, liberating his own and paving the way for his kingdom.

Looking for Salvation and Missing the Savior

Prophecies concerning the first and second comings of Jesus, the messiah, the promised seed, abound throughout scripture. We've already looked at a few. Here are some others to chew on.

Moses wrote these prophetic words:

> I see him, but not now;
> I behold him, but not near.
> A star will come out of Jacob;
> a scepter will rise out of Israel
> (Numbers 24:17a NIV).

Some seven hundred years before the birth of Christ in Bethlehem, Isaiah predicted:

> For a child will be born to us, a son will be
> given to us;

And the government will rest on His shoulders;
And His name will be called Wonderful Counselor,
Mighty God,
Eternal Father, Prince of Peace.
There will be no end to the increase of His
government or of peace,
On the throne of David and over his kingdom,
To establish it and to uphold it with justice and
righteousness
From then on and forevermore.
The zeal of the Lord of hosts will accomplish
this (Isaiah 9:6-7 NASB).

A contemporary of Isaiah recorded the birthplace of the messiah, 750 years before it took place. God got specific in detailing the name of the small town, Bethlehem, where the savior's first coming would occur and he graciously revealed this news to a simple, unassuming villager named Micah, who wrote down a birth announcement for posterity:

But you, Bethlehem Ephrathah,
though you are small among the clans of Judah,
out of you will come for me
one who will be ruler over Israel,
whose origins are from old,
from ancient times (Micah 5:2 NIV).

And, writing some six hundred years before the birth of Christ, the weeping prophet, Jeremiah, recorded this revelation from the Lord:

"The days are coming," declares the Lord,
"when I will raise up to David a righteous
Branch,
a King who will reign wisely
and do what is just and right in the land.

In his days Judah will be saved
   and Israel will live in safety.
This is the name by which he will be called:
   The Lord Our Righteousness"
(Jeremiah 23:5-6 NIV).

Those prophecies, which are only a few of hundreds concerning the first and second advents of Christ, stir the heart and mind. They depict, in part, the triumphant return of the savior, the second coming of the king of kings to set up his eternal domain. Reading them, it is easy to conceive of Christ's royalty, divinity, and majesty. It is also easy to forget his humanity. That is what the Israelites did so long ago. On Palm Sunday, most of them looked for a king above all kings as Jesus rode into Jerusalem. They anticipated a liberator; they were given a savior who would suffer for their sakes. They looked for the messiah to come with sword brandished and gleaming, calling all to arms, a political activist able to pull strings in private to bring about public results. They didn't realize that he would first conquer through the cross, although that too was prophesied in his Father's word (see Isaiah 52:13–53:12).

Looking for a conqueror and overlooking a king—such was the mind-set of the people of Israel as the Palm Sunday account opens. Into his city the Lord came, but inside his city the prince of this world, Satan, had already actively anticipated the king's arrival and had blinded the eyes of his subjects.

Satan, who rebelled and fell from a lofty position of honor because of that rebellion (Ezekiel 28:12ff), who offered the kingdoms of this world to Christ in Matthew 4, still blinds eyes today. Grasping for Satan's materialism, we forget the master. Looking for the type of savior we expect, we overlook the one who has already come to do the work of salvation. Like the people of Israel, we search for the Christ of our own conjecture, without recognizing that he has already arrived, a baby born in Bethlehem, a carpenter's son grown to manhood in Nazareth.

Let's now journey back to that day when the Lord entered what should have been his capital city of Jerusalem and offered himself to his own. Five hundred years before Easter week, the prophet Zechariah wrote these words, which God had revealed to him. They describe in surprising detail the episode we're about to consider, the coming of Israel's king:

> Rejoice greatly, O Daughter of Zion!
> Shout, Daughter of Jerusalem!
> See, your king comes to you,
> righteous and having salvation,
> gentle and riding on a donkey,
> on a colt, the foal of a donkey
> (Zechariah 9:9 NIV).

And Zechariah continued:

> I will take away the chariots from Ephraim
> and the war-horses from Jerusalem,
> and the battle bow will be broken.
> He will proclaim peace to the nations.
> His rule will extend from sea to sea
> and from the River to the ends of the earth
> (Zechariah 9:10 NIV).

The first portion of Zechariah's prophecy, verse 9, is a portrait of Palm Sunday. It's what we see as we peruse the gospels. Verse 10 is a prediction of Christ's glorious return.

In our longing for salvation, may we not make the mistake of the Jews of A.D. 29 in Jerusalem. May we never overlook the gentleness of a savior astride a donkey, coming first in peace and humility. May we never forget the certainty of the return of a triumphant king. As Paul put it later in his letter to Titus:

> For the grace of God has appeared, bringing salvation to all men, instructing us to deny ungodliness and worldly

> desires and to live sensibly, righteously and godly in the present age, looking for the blessed hope and the appearing of the glory of our great God and Savior, Christ Jesus (Titus 2:11-13 NASB).

Friday and Saturday

Let's pick up the pre-Palm Sunday action. It's Friday. In anticipation of the Passover, the most important feast on the Jewish calendar, Jesus and his men journeyed northward from Jericho to the city of Bethany, a small town some two miles east of Jerusalem. They retraced the route taken centuries before by the Israelites who followed Joshua into the promised land. Among those accompanying Christ to Bethany were two men from the outskirts of Jericho whose blindness he had cured with the touch of his hand (Matthew 20:30-34). Somewhere along the way, James and John made the power play for key seats in the kingdom, described in Mark 10 (10:33-45).

On Friday evening, the beginning of the Jewish sabbath, Jesus and company stopped in Bethany at one of their favorite spots, the home of Mary, Martha, and Lazarus. He and the disciples were frequent, always welcomed, guests of this trio of sisters and brother, and they spent Friday night and all day Saturday in Bethany, celebrating the sabbath. This was the same Lazarus whom Christ earlier called forth from the grave in John 11.

What a woman Martha was. Organized, energetic, opinionated—she was burdened by busyness. She needed to "be still and know that I am God." That was the hardest verse in the Bible for her (Psalm 46:10). Despite her faults, you'd have liked her. The warmth of her love radiated through her personality and like a magnet drew people close. She made them feel at home, although she worked her fingers to the bone doing it. You know others like Martha, don't you? They serve on committees, direct clubs and single-handedly run kitchens at church dinners. Martha was in her element serving supper to a crowd, and this sabbath meal at her neighbor Simon's home was no different.

Martha shifted into high gear when the Lord came to call, but her sister Mary did otherwise. Wherever we see her in scripture, Mary focused on the savior, refusing to be swept into a whirlwind of activity. During one of the Lord's earlier visits, much to the chagrin of Martha, Mary sat listening at the feet of Jesus instead of flying about the kitchen helping with meal preparation (Luke 10:38ff).

The next time we see the pair in the gospels, Martha scolded the Lord because he had not arrived in time to save Lazarus from dying. While Martha chided, Mary sat quietly waiting for Jesus. When he summoned her, she immediately came, falling at his feet and shedding tears because of the loss of her beloved brother (see John 11:1-46). Now, on the eve of Christ's entry into Jerusalem, it was as if Mary sensed the trauma of the week ahead. While Martha served supper, Mary took a flask of costly perfume and broke it open. With the fragrance she anointed the feet of Jesus, and gently wiped them with her hair. Her act of worship infuriated Judas, who alleged that it was a waste of money, and in whose heart the seeds of betrayal had already taken root (see Matthew 26:6ff; Mark 14:3ff; John 12:1-9).

Sunday Morning

Then dawned the morning of a day like no other, the first twenty-four hours of a week like no other. The sun rose on Sunday, and excitement crackled in the air. The enthusiasm was contagious. Yes, Jesus had been to Jerusalem many times before, but today his entry would be unique. He would come as the prophet Zechariah revealed he would, in peace and astride a colt (Zechariah 9:9; see also Isaiah 9:6). In offering himself officially to the Hebrew nation as its king, he would elicit the hostility and animosity of the Jewish religious leaders already consumed with jealousy. His popularity would force the Sanhedrin, the Jewish governing body, to deal with him immediately, rather than to wait for the close of the Passover as they had intended (see Matthew 26:5). As Jesus prepared to enter the city, he knew he would be riding to his death.

And When They Drew Near

Matthew 21 begins with these words: "And when they had approached Jerusalem and had come to Bethphage, to the Mount of Olives, then Jesus sent two disciples" (NASB). From the home of Mary, Martha, and Lazarus, Jesus and his followers walked the dusty two miles toward Jerusalem.

"And when they had approached Jerusalem . . ." Pause for a moment and consider those words. The phrase "and when" emphasizes that God's sovereign hand was behind all the events. "My hour has not yet come" were words that Jesus often spoke during his earthly pilgrimage, but now there was a change. It hadn't been time for his public offering of himself until now. Of this week, he said that his hour was at hand (see John 13:1; 17:1; see also Galatians 4:4-5). The humanly unknown would soon become known. The *ifs* in the minds of the disciples would now turn to *whens*. The king would enter his capital as a king, at last.

Bethphage, where the entourage paused, was evidently a small village between Bethany and Jerusalem. Nonexistent today, its name means "house of unripe figs," and how aptly that description fits those waiting within the walls of Jerusalem. They were as unprepared for Christ's coming as unripe figs are to be harvested. At Bethphage the Lord turned to two of his disciples and issued this command:

> Go into the village opposite you, and immediately you will find a donkey tied there and a colt with her; untie them, and bring them to Me. And if anyone says something to you, you shall say, "The Lord has need of them," and immediately he will send them (Matthew 21:2-3 NASB).

Jesus didn't ask for volunteers at Bethphage. He turned to two of the twelve and simply said, "Go . . . untie . . . bring." In telling them how to answer anyone who would object to their taking the donkey and colt, he called himself, for the first time, "the Lord." To him belonged power and authority, and so he announced who he was. Christ's presentation of himself to his people would be as unpretentious as his birth. Born among animals in a stable, he would now be borne into Jerusalem on the back of a beast of burden. Why? As Matthew went on to reveal, with his command Christ showed us his full awareness of the prophetic word:

> Now this took place that what was spoken through the prophet might be fulfilled, saying,
> "Say to the daughter of Zion,
> 'Behold, your king is coming to you,
> Gentle, and mounted on a donkey,
> Even on a colt, the foal of a beast of burden' "
> (Matthew 21:4-5 NASB).

Event after event of Easter week would fulfill scripture spoken hundreds of years earlier. As Zechariah had predicted, on the back of the colt of a donkey the king would present himself to the "daughter of Zion," the inhabitants of Jerusalem. In peace he came, and in humility. Had he chosen a horse, his intentions would have seemed warlike. Instead, in accordance with scripture, he selected a donkey, an animal also used by royalty at times, but one that would not convey images of challenge, conflict, and combat.

How did the disciples respond to Christ's orders at Bethphage? We read that they "went and did just as Jesus had directed them, and brought the donkey and the colt, and laid on them their garments, on which He sat" (Matthew 21:6-7 NASB). Surely it seemed odd to them to be asked to walk into a strange village and commandeer a donkey and foal. They had to be thinking to themselves, "What is Jesus up to? What does he want? Why is he asking us to do this? Couldn't we just *buy* a donkey? What if the owners stop us?"

But whatever they might have thought, the disciples went where the Lord wanted them to go. They did what he wanted them to do. (No surer recipe for happiness exists anywhere.) They returned with the donkey and its foal, and Jesus mounted the colt and continued the journey.

Hosannas to the Son

Two hundred years before Jesus rode into Jerusalem, a great Jewish hero named Judas the Maccabee cleansed the temple and was greeted by throngs of men, women, and children shouting loud hosannas. The account is found in the apocryphal book of 2 Maccabees. Before that, when Jehu became king of Israel, 2 Kings 9:13 tells us that the people removed their cloaks and spread them in his path. Amid trumpet blasts the cry resounded, "Jehu is king!" A no less royal welcome greeted Jesus Christ as he neared Jerusalem.

In his path the multitudes spread garments on the road. Others cut branches from nearby trees and laid them before him (Matthew 21:8). The swelling crowds, pressing close to him, running before him, following after him, were heard to cry:

> Hosanna to the Son of David;
> Blessed is he who comes in the name of the Lord;
> Hosanna in the highest! (Matthew 21:9 NASB).

Today we use the term *hosanna* as we would some exclamation like "hallelujah," "amen," or "praise the Lord." Yet the original root meaning of the word is this: "Save now, I pray thee!" It's a combination of prayer and praise, and when you think about it, the implications are heavy. The multitudes shouting in his path and in his wake were calling for Christ to save them. That was his intention, but not in the way they expected. They weren't looking for freedom from their sin, but rather for deliverance from the rule of the Roman empire. They expected the messiah to blaze into town, muster his troops, and lead a revolt against Roman oppression. They looked for him to set up the kingdom that had been promised, and for which they had desperately prayed.

And to whom did they shout hosanna? Notice that the crowds called Jesus the "Son of David." He possessed all the credentials of the Christ. He had a right to rule and reign unrivaled on his eternal throne. He was the promised messiah. But he came to a nation grown spiritually cold. He offered himself to a people who would not see him for who he was.

It is interesting that in Luke's account of the triumphal entry, as the throngs of people shouted with joy at Christ's entry, the Pharisees or Jewish religious leaders responded to the chorus of hosannas by imploring Jesus to silence the crowds. "Teacher, rebuke Your disciples" (Luke 19:39 NASB). In other words, "Jesus, tell them to be quiet. Make them stop." What was the Lord's reply? Turning to the Pharisees, he answered, "I tell you, if these become silent, the stones will cry out!" (Luke 19:40 NASB). The hosannas were going to be heard, one way or another. If the people remained quiet, then the stones would voice the chorus.

Even nature sings praises of its creator. The winds blow a tune in a minor key; the waves crash ashore in splendor; the trees clap their hands. Yet the glorious entry would soon be over, and shortly we'll see the awful and awesome results of our Lord's obedient humanity.

Within the Eastern Gate

Down off the slopes of the mount of Olives, the swelling, singing throng walked into the Kidron valley, passing vineyards and the gnarled olive trees of Gethsemane. Upward to Jerusalem the pulsating mass climbed, mounting the gently ascending slopes, marching into the city through its eastern gate.

That gate is forever closed now, until that day when the messiah returns to establish his eternal throne. One of the most meaningful experiences I've ever had on trips to the holy land happened on our first tour there. Pearl and I stood outside the closed eastern gate, and looked across the Kidron valley to the slopes of the mount of Olives. From this panoramic viewing spot, in my mind's eye I could not only see Palm Sunday, but also the glorious future day of Christ's return, his soon coming. The longing of our hearts is, Lord Jesus, come quickly! Our joy will know no bounds when at last our savior is seated on the throne of his kingdom.

Into the city of Jerusalem, Christ rode, surrounded by the masses. We read that "when He had entered Jerusalem, all the city was stirred, saying, 'Who is this?' " (Matthew 21:10 NASB). The Greek word used to describe the fact that the entire city was "stirred" is the same from which we derive our word *seismic*. We're talking about a major upheaval of Richter scale proportions. The running of the bulls at Pamplona is minor compared to this stampede of humanity. According to the Hebrew historian Josephus, there were probably 2.5 million people in the city of Jerusalem celebrating the Passover. Every Jew within a twenty-mile radius was required to come. Thousands of these drifted into the procession accompanying Christ.

Why had they come? From where? A vast host had undoubtedly followed Jesus north from Jericho in the first place. Multitudes had heard of the raising of Lazarus, and now pressed for a glimpse of the one who could command corpses to breathe again. Hundreds probably poured in from regions like Galilee and Berea, where news of Jesus' miracles had spread like wildfire. They came—the curious, the skeptical, the conniving, the convinced—to see him. They were salesmen, soldiers, housewives, engineers, laborers, slaves, tax collectors, prostitutes. Some were pious, some pagan, some zealous, some ambitious, some just plain scared. Their common ground? A quest to see him.

"Who is this?" The question about Christ's identity was

raised in the shaken city. And the reply given by many in the burgeoning crowd was, "This is the prophet Jesus, from Nazareth in Galilee" (Matthew 21:11).

Their words leave me cold. What about you? The throngs pressing close saw only a prophet, perhaps a human king. They had no inkling that he was their savior, their high priest who would offer the ultimate sacrifice for their salvation. They did not recognize that he was the lamb of God, come to take away the sin of the world. Seeking their own style of majesty, they missed the master.

Even Jesus' own disciples, his chosen ones, became so caught up in the intensity of the royal entrance that they missed the master too. All week they jockeyed for positions in his cabinet. They even spent their last meal with the Lord arguing about who would be first in his kingdom, their hearts proud, their feet dirty till he washed them. Thursday night they dined with him in the upper room. On Friday he would be dead, and although he explained this to them, they were still swept away by visions of grandeur and glory (see Luke 9:44-46).

By the time Friday rolled around, the only ones still calling him king were the Roman soldiers who did so to mock him, this "King of the Jews." They draped a scarlet robe across his back, raw with gaping wounds from the whipping he received with the cat-o'-nine-tails. They pressed a stick into his hand as a ridiculous scepter and smashed a crown of thorns onto his scalp. He was beaten, rebuked, spat on. The reed that once was his mock scepter became a club and was used to slap him. Later in the day, nails punctured his hands and feet. As he hung on the cross, a crudely lettered banner grotesquely proclaimed his royalty only as a joke to a world watching him die (see Matthew 27:27-37).

The Offer Made

For now, though, the offer had been made. As Jesus rode into Jerusalem, we see the formal presentation of a king to his people. We witness the official offer of the messiah to those he came to save. We'll soon observe their rejection of him, with all its glorious and grievous implications. It was Israel's last chance as a nation to respond to its king.

Luke tells us in his gospel that as Christ approached the city, he wept, saying of Jerusalem and her inhabitants, "If you had known in this day, even you, the things which make for peace! But now they have been hidden from your eyes" (19:41-42 NASB). Later Jesus lamented over the lost condition of his people. They had not seen him as he was, for who he was. "O Jerusalem, Jerusalem, who kills the prophets and stones those who are sent to her!" the Lord exclaimed with aching sorrow. "How often I wanted to gather your children together, the way a hen gathers her chicks under her wings, and you were unwilling. Behold, your house is being left to you desolate!" (Matthew 23:37-38 NASB).

The offer tendered was the offer refused. His heart breaking, the Lord turned from Israel and its faithless authorities and said with indescribable sadness, "For I say to you, from now on you shall not see Me until you say, 'Blessed is he who comes in the name of the Lord!' " (Matthew 23:39 NASB). Individuals might still come to him in faith, but the nation of Israel had rejected him.

Tying It Together

We've seen the Sunday welcome. Soon we'll observe a nation's change of heart. What does it all mean to us, on this side of the cross?

First, what ought to come through loud and clear is that God never breaks a promise. Psalm 89:33-34 says of the Lord's covenant with David, "But I will not take my love from him, nor will I ever betray my faithfulness. I will not betray my covenant or alter what my lips have uttered" (NIV). When God says it, he'll do it, and we'd better believe it. Even though the Jews rejected him, he would still keep his promises to David.

There would still be an eternal throne, from which Jesus Christ, Son of David, would rule and reign. Ample verses in scripture support this truth. Here are a few:

> The kingdom of the world has become the kingdom of our Lord, and of His Christ; and He will reign forever and ever (Revelation 11:15b NASB).

> Now the salvation, and the power, and the kingdom of our God and the authority of His Christ have come, for the accuser of our brethren has been thrown down, who accuses them before our God day and night (Revelation 12:10 NASB).

We witnessed Christ's first triumphal coming into his capital city, a procession fulfilling biblical prophecy to the letter. The reality of his first entry should convince us that his second will take place too. The Bible doesn't contain false speculations. God doesn't lie. The Son is going to come again.

What about us, in the meantime? While we await the kingdom, we should realize that God has delegated some responsibilities to us. We have free will. There is a throne within each of our hearts. We can choose to let darkness rule there, or we can choose to open ourselves to the kingdom of light. God is knocking at the door of our hearts (Revelation 3:20). He is asking to enter the gates of our souls. He is waiting and watching to witness our responses.

Do we, like Jerusalem, reject him?

Or do we allow him to reign?

Focusing the Lens

Something amazing happened to the number-one agnostic in our church at Hide-A-Way Lake a few months ago. A seventy-year-old supremely self-confident man finally came to grips with the truth about Jesus Christ. Les had been a delightful skeptic: polite, astutely British, intellectual. For years we'd hashed and rehashed scripture. We good-naturedly argued. His wife diligently prayed. But still Les wouldn't be convinced. He'd come to church once in a while with friends, but he'd never let any of the messages get to him personally. It was nice that his wife found such comfort in her religion, but he didn't need it. He could afford to stay aloof.

You couldn't help but like him. He was a wonderful man, a good man, a pleasant man—but he was also a condemned man, in the eyes of God.

Then finally one day it all came together. Les describes the experience in his own words:

> I was a hypocrite. I acted like a Christian, but I was not. I have likened my thoughts to that of a camera that would not focus. Therefore, all my views were fuzzy and unclear. I looked for God in the wrong places such as Judaism and even Islamic cults. While listening to a sermon one day, it all suddenly became clear. I prayed silently for Christ to come into my heart, and he did. Right then, my lens was in focus.
>
> I have never had a doubt since that day. My life has changed, so much so that I can hardly believe that I could ever have doubted. The Lord has changed me, and my wife and associates see the difference in me and testify to it. I love my Lord and I know he loves me, and has forgiven me.

Like Les, is your spiritual lens fuzzy and unclear? Are you looking for answers in all the wrong places? Maybe even considering cults, eastern religions, EST, meditation, scientology? Thinking about checking into spiritual mediums and channelers? If so, it's time to focus the lens. It's time to key in on the only answer: Jesus Christ. Before you embrace the exotic, why not consider the claims of Christ this Easter? Objectively look in your own backyard, before running to the writings of Buddha or Mohammed, Sun Myung Moon or Joseph Smith. Think about specific prophecies fulfilled to the letter in the life, death, and resurrection of Christ Jesus. Levi, Reuben, and Joshua, can you step out in courage and make a stand? He is the lamb to end all sacrifices.

You owe it to yourself not to overlook his message a single season longer. You are invited, as was the nation of Israel nearly two thousand years ago, to behold your king.

Reflections for the season

1. Read again Zechariah 9:9 and Matthew 21:1-11, and note the striking similarities. They are more than mere coincidence. It is said that what Jesus Christ has done in history seals what he will do. Explain this in your own words. What difference, if any, does it make in your life?

2. Do you know anyone like Martha, the sister of Mary and Lazarus? Think of situations in your own life where it may be tough for you to listen as the Lord says, "Be still, and know that I am God." Determine now to spend extra time reading and meditating on his word when the busyness reaches fever pitch. When you desire to get to know God more deeply, you'll be amazed at the extra minutes you'll find to do just that.

3. Pause and consider the kind of savior you're seeking. Are you looking for a God who will perform on your command—curing your physical ills, healing your shattered family, solving your financial woes? Are you searching for someone to make you healthy, wealthy, and wise, and otherwise shower you with a hassle-free existence? The Lord never promises that we'll avoid the fiery furnace, only that he'll take us through the trauma. Be certain you're not looking for the Christ of your own conjecture, as were the people of Israel two thousand years ago.

C H A P T E R T H R E E

The Suffering Servant

Isaiah 52:13-53:12

On a couple of occasions I have had the privilege of speaking at the annual Bible conference of Hillcrest Baptist Church in St. John, New Brunswick. The quaint town is pure delight to visit, and the people are a joy. They love their lobsters and fiddleheads. The Bay of Fundy rises and falls with each tide. Severe Canadian winters create a rugged stamina in the folks there, and this toughness spills over into the depth of spiritual commitment made by those who have received Jesus Christ. I've seldom seen such determination to grow.

I think of Mae Todd, who at seventy-five years of age trudged a mile on foot through deep snow just to make it to Bible class, and later wrote that she had learned from the conference to "grasp the importance of guarding my times alone with Jesus in the study of his word and in prayer." Judging from her dedication, I think Mae had already figured all that out long before I stepped into the pulpit.

While in St. John seven years ago, someone pressed a news article into my hand and urged me to read it. Its first words captured the Canadian spirit and convinced me to continue. "Once in a while there appears an exceptional human being whose words and deeds restore faith in the human race . . .

who fills us lesser mortals with pride to be a member of the species." So began the article from the *Vancouver Sun.*

The accolades were for Terry Fox, a young Canadian cancer victim who set out to run a marathon of hope across his country in order to raise money for research on the treacherous disease. At the beginning of his quest, Terry's optimism shone brightly as he announced, "Anything is possible. If everyone in Canada gave just one dollar, we would have twenty-four million for cancer research. Dreams are made if people only try." For 3,339 miles Terry tried valiantly to live out his dream, running on his one real and one artificial leg, until a resurgence of his cancer forced him to cease on September 1, 1980. He never completed his marathon of hope, but on December 5 of that same year the Cancer Society announced plans for a million-dollar research laboratory, to be funded with money raised through Terry's efforts.

At that news conference, in a quiet voice, Terry Fox announced that the doctors had given him a ten percent chance of survival. Quietly, haltingly, courageously, Terry explained that when death became imminent, he knew he would have to face it, accept it, and trust God in it to relieve the loneliness. The tragic epilogue to the story is that Terry Fox did succumb to the disease he had bravely battled, slipping into eternity in June 1981.

Would We Measure Up?

Our human heroes, the Terry Foxes we encounter—their deeds stir the soul. Reading about them brings butterflies to the stomach, a lump to the throat, tears to the eyes. And well it should. Intellectually we tell ourselves that these folks are ordinary men and women made extraordinary through their circumstances. Yet in the midst of our rational thought, perhaps each of us faintly wonders if under similar conditions we'd measure up. Could we pull it off? Do we have what it takes?

Would we be like William of Orange, who on the eve of a perilous undertaking stoically wrote the following to Anne of Saxony, "I go tomorrow, but when I shall return or when I shall see you, I cannot, on my honor, tell you with certainty. I have resolved to place myself in the hands of the almighty, that he may guide me whither it is his good pleasure that I should go"?

Would we be like Corrie ten Boom, who, two weeks after the death of her beloved sister Betsie in the Nazi concentration camp where they were confined, was unexpectedly called forth from the ranks of prisoners at roll call? Such undue attention usually meant bad news. For three hours Corrie stood in line with the others who'd been singled out, shivering in the icy December chill.

"Why am I here?" Corrie whispered to the young girl next to her in line.

"Death sentence," came the somber reply.

Standing in the frigid valley of the shadow, Corrie could well have been crippled by terrors of the unknown, rendered mute while mental hobgoblins of gas chambers and crematoriums danced in her head. But facing the prospect of death, she was neither paralyzed by fear nor consumed with self. She began to tell the girl beside her of the warmth of the love of Jesus, the unconditional, unending love that death could not destroy, but only make complete. For what seemed at the time to be their final hours of life, the young girl and the other prisoners in line listened intently to a brave older woman who was unafraid to die (Brown 64).

Would we be Terry Foxes? Would we be Corrie ten Booms? Would we hurl ourselves in front of an oncoming subway train to knock a wandering toddler off the tracks? Would we surrender our seat in the lifeboat if there weren't enough room for all? Would we crawl out of the foxhole to assist a wounded buddy while enemy bullets whizzed about? Would we relinquish a kidney to save a dying sister? Would we courageously accept the negative results of a catscan, biopsy, or blood test, and calmly begin to prepare our loved ones for our own departure? In defending our Christian faith, would we face the stones with the confidence of Stephen? Would we endure the spears, the executioner's axe, the flames, the boiling oil? Could we exclaim to God, with the martyred missionary, "Blood is only of value as it flows before thine altars"?

Would we be heroes? All of us have to answer that question on our own. For many of us, I'd like to think the answer is yes. Humankind does rise to the occasion. The ordinary quite often is transformed into the extraordinary. On the other hand, we're notorious for sinking to baser levels too. Often we selfishly opt to seek satisfaction in the here and now. We focus on what we can get, not on what we can give. We choose health, wealth, and prosperity over sacrifice, service, and sainthood.

The Courage of Calvary

Another issue arises when we think of the sacrifices made by others. We view feats of human unselfishness as strangely majestic. Self-sacrificing heroes never fail to arouse our admiration; tales of their accomplishments and courage tug at our hearts and open the floodgates of our eyes. And what I am about to say should in no way be seen as an attempt to diminish the significance of the Terry Foxes, the Corrie ten Booms, the Williams of Orange. Yet the fact remains that it is ironic, even incomprehensible, why stories of the sacrificial actions of men and women move us so deeply, while the account of the sacrifice of Christ at Calvary often leaves us cold.

Think about Terry Fox and you heave a sigh of wonder. Read a hymn about Christ, and the result probably won't be the same.

> Lifted up was He to die,
> "It is finished," was His cry;

Now in heaven exalted high;
Hallelujah! what a Saviour!
(Philip P. Bliss)

It doesn't do the same for you, does it? Why don't we gasp in awe at the sacrifice of Jesus? Why don't tears stream from our eyes at the thought of the cost of Calvary? Why don't lumps fill our throats when we read of his wondrous love?

Why? I don't really know. Perhaps we're used to it. We've heard about the cross since we were children, and the first few times the story may have affected us, but now we're desensitized. We've grown callous and compassionless. It's old hat to us. Since nowadays executions are at midnight in isolated prison chambers, it could be that the concept of a public crucifixion is too foreign to us. Maybe we don't fully understand what happened on that hill outside Jerusalem. Maybe we haven't genuinely grasped that in his thirty-three years on earth, Christ was totally God and *totally man.* Yes, omnipotent God hung on a cross, but a man also dangled there, a man of flesh, blood, bones, sinew; a man who felt searing pain, who ached as his muscles were torn, whose joints throbbed as they were stretched asunder; a man who was God, who didn't have to die, who could have summoned an angelic army to his rescue—he is the one who let the soldiers pound nails into his hands and feet and fasten him to the rough-hewn beams. May we never again be guilty of viewing his sacrifice coldly or complacently.

A Well-Planned Memorial

At the last supper which he shared with his disciples before Calvary, Jesus took the bread, gave thanks, and broke it, saying, "This is My body which is given for you; do this in remembrance of Me." He next took a cup, and with these words offered it to his followers, "This cup which is poured out for you is the new covenant in My blood" (Luke 22:19-20

NASB). This do in *remembrance* of me, the savior said. May the Lord stir up our minds in remembrance. May we neither forget his battered body and shed blood, nor ever take them for granted.

To keep us from growing cold about Calvary, in the next two chapters of this book we're going to look at two passages of scripture that depict the cross in all its intensity. They're gripping photographs, burning images straight from the sacred page. Curiously, neither of the passages was written by a contemporary of Christ. Neither writer was an eyewitness of the crucifixion; neither had ever even heard about that form of execution. Each simply recorded what the Lord, through the Holy Spirit, revealed to him, centuries before the described events ever took place.

King David was the author of Psalm 22, the second of the passages we'll consider, and the more vividly descriptive of the agonies of the cross. We'll look first at the words of the prophet Isaiah, chapters 52:13–53:12 of his book, a section that many people consider the peak of Old Testament prophecy.

Polycarp, bishop of Smyrna and disciple of the apostle John, called Isaiah 53 the "golden passional." The text was recommended reading by Martin Luther, who urged other believers to commit it to memory. When the apostle Philip hitchhiked a ride with the Ethiopian eunuch in Acts 8, it was Isaiah 53 that the eunuch was poring over and which he asked Philip to explain. When I preach on the passage, I title my message "The Humiliation and Glorification of Jehovah's Servant"; that's what it's all about. It's Christ as God's servant, Christ dying, Christ glorified.

How do we know that Isaiah 52:13–53:12 was written about Christ? When the Ethiopian eunuch implored Philip to clarify the verses, Acts 8:35 tells us that Philip "opened his mouth, and beginning from this Scripture he preached Jesus to him" (NASB). Jesus himself quoted part of the passage in

John 12:38, in reference to himself. The apostle Paul spoke of Isaiah 52:15 in connection with the gospel of Christ (Romans 15:21). That Isaiah 53 is a snapshot of Calvary will become obvious as we turn to that scripture.

The text is so real, so relevant, so descriptive of the life and death of Jesus Christ that it's easy to forget when it was written. Isaiah lived seven hundred years before Jesus was born. There was no Roman empire then, no crucifixion. From the beginning of his prophetic ministry around 750 B.C., Isaiah looked for the messiah; God gave him truths to record about the messiah, but he never shook Jesus' hand; he never touched his face. Yet he saw Christ's destiny and wrote about it with incredible precision. Who but God's Spirit could have revealed the future to Isaiah in such detail? Awareness of the undeniable hand of the supernatural ought to grip us as we read.

And here's something else to think about as we look at what Isaiah has to say. In this life, the acts of human nobility, of human self-sacrifice, of human unselfishness, which we so admire, are very often spontaneous. Very often, not always, they are the results of decisions made on the spur of the moment. I'm talking about the heroics of the young mother who leaps a fence to pull a vicious guard dog off her youngster; the plane crash victim who sinks in choppy coastal waters after helping a fellow passenger grasp a rescue helicopter's ladder; the uncle who runs back into the blistering heat of a smoke- and fire-filled building to search for a niece from whom he's been separated in the melee. Spontaneity often characterizes our heroism, and certainly makes it no less heroic. Yet what if we had time to think about it first? What if we had time to ponder each gruesome detail of the suffering we'd endure while being heroic? Be honest with yourself. If you knew that the ocean liner was going to collide with an iceberg and you were going to sink to a watery grave while helping to hoist others into crowded lifeboats, would you ever get on board the ship? The legacy of the *Titanic* is not without its heroes, but I doubt any would have set sail had they foreknown its fate. I would have stayed ashore, I assure you.

And yet Christ knew.

Christ boarded the ship.

Christ accepted the cross.

Jesus knew all about the suffering beforehand—every detail, every moment. He knew about it because he is God. The biblical words of David and Isaiah originated with him. No excruciating element was hidden from him. He'd memorized the play-by-play before the game began.

He came to earth anyway.

That he loved us enough to do that is among the miracles of Calvary.

The Destiny of the Servant—Isaiah 52:13-15

> See, my servant will act wisely;
> he will be raised and lifted up and highly exalted.
> Just as there were many who were appalled at him—
> his appearance was so disfigured beyond that of any man
> and his form marred beyond human likeness—
> so will he sprinkle many nations,
> and kings will shut their mouths because of him.
> For what they were not told, they will see,
> and what they have not heard, they will understand (NIV).

As we turn to the words of Isaiah, we're going to first look at the end of chapter 52, before we plunge into chapter 53. The whole passage, from 52:13–53:12, is like a hymn that can be broken into five stanzas of three verses each, centering on these truths about the ultimate servant, Christ Jesus:

His destiny . . . 52:13-15
His career . . . 53:1-3
His suffering . . . 53:4-6
His obedience . . .53:7-9
His reward . . . 53:10-12

It's important to realize that in Isaiah 52:13-15, the Lord Jehovah, God the Father, is speaking. This brief section serves as an introduction to chapter 53. God is revealing the plot ahead of time, giving us a preview of what's ahead. Basically, the Lord is telling us what he's going to tell us, and when he repeats ideas or concepts in scripture, it's a surefire signal to pay attention.

His exaltation. God speaks first of the exaltation of his servant, the Christ. "See, my servant will act wisely; he will be raised and lifted up and highly exalted" (52:13 NIV). According to the Father, Christ will be elevated to a position of honor and glory.

Who will exalt Christ? Humanly speaking, exaltation is the Father's department. Psalm 75:6-7 puts it this way, "No one from the east or the west or from the desert can exalt a man. But it is God who judges: He brings one down, he exalts another" (NIV). 1 Peter 5:5-6 urges, "All of you, clothe yourselves with humility toward one another, for God is opposed to the proud, but gives grace to the humble. Humble yourselves, therefore, under the mighty hand of God, that He may exalt you at the proper time" (NASB). As the elevation of men and women to positions of honor is the business of the Father, so is the exaltation of the Son.

Philippians 2:9-11 tells us more, as we read Paul's words about the aftermath of Jesus' death on the cross:

> Therefore also God highly exalted Him, and bestowed on Him that name which is above every name, that at the name of Jesus every knee should bow . . . and that every

> tongue should confess that Jesus Christ is Lord, to the glory of God the Father (NASB).

In Ephesians 1:20-23, Paul put it this way:

> He brought about in Christ, when He raised Him from the dead, and seated Him at His right hand in the heavenly places, far above all rule and authority and power and dominion, and every name that is named, not only in this age, but also in the one to come. And He put all things in subjection under His feet, and gave Him as head over all things to the church, which is His body, the fulness of Him who fills all in all (NASB).

These verses teach us that following his crucifixion, death, resurrection, and ascension, Christ was exalted by the Father, who seated the Son at his right hand in heaven. Only part of the business of exalting the Son has been accomplished. Some remains unfinished. Specifically, the day is yet to come when *every* knee will bow and *every* tongue confess that Jesus is Lord. The moment in which Christ's enemies will be made a footstool for his feet will take place as the Father clears the way by putting down all resistance and rebellion, and by executing judgment. Then our hearts will sing the "Battle Hymn of the Republic"; our eyes will see "the glory of the coming of the Lord." We'll watch the "fateful lightning of His terrible swift sword." His truth will march on in a day of victory and vindication for the Son.

Why will the Father exalt the Son? It is because Jesus perfectly accomplished everything his heavenly Father asked of him. As Isaiah 52:13 states, he acted "wisely," never sinning in thirty-three years of human existence. He never cheated, told a lie, uttered gossip, flew off the handle unreasonably, put his own desires ahead of those of others. Gentle, kind, and consistent, he never once wavered in his mission. When angry, his anger was righteous, was motivated by the "religious" world's blatant disregard for his Father, and was reserved for the Jewish leaders who'd long before lost their first love. He would cleanse the temple and verbally splatter shots at the Pharisees, but he never turned on anyone in tiredness. He never came apart under the stress of the moment. He never was in a hurry; he never was anxious, or late. He was never afraid that the Father wouldn't be faithful to him. He never grew bitter and resentful. He didn't play politics so he could get control. He never stayed up late evaluating his performance and setting selfish goals. Personal prosperity never entered his mind; he knew that the Father cares for his own.

The Lord Jesus embodied wisdom. He personified the character of God. Twice in the gospel of Matthew, the Father stated of him, "This is my beloved Son, in whom I am well pleased" (see Matthew 3:17; 17:5). He is worthy of glory and praise and exaltation. Worship, honor, and respect are fitting tributes to the king of kings.

Yet it's worth noting that Jesus didn't see his mission on earth as a highway to heavenly reward. He didn't dwell on the glory he would gain. He wasn't puffed up, proud, egotistical, or ambitious. As he said of himself, "For even the Son of Man did not come to be served, but to serve, and to give His life a ransom for many" (Mark 10:45 NASB).

He came to serve, to teach, to heal, to wash the feet of his disciples—and to yield to the cross. His was a service of suffering.

His suffering. The torment, this suffering of the Christ, is what Isaiah next graphically foretold in his text. "Just as there were many who were appalled at him—his appearance was so disfigured beyond that of any man and his form marred beyond human likeness" (Isaiah 52:14).

Conjure in your mind pictures of human horror and deprivation. Auschwitz, Bergen-Belsen, Hiroshima, Nagasaki, Bangladesh, Biafra, Cambodia, Iwo Jima, Vietnam—those names of the notorious evoke mental images of wasted limbs, emaciated torsos, empty eyes, seared flesh, festering wounds.

Staring blankly from behind the cold barbed wire of a concentration camp, joints protruding, faces gaunt, the rag-clad prisoners appear shockingly spectral. So do the malnourished children of Third World countries who've become hapless, helpless pawns of political upheaval. Bellies swelling, matchstick legs and arms, faces too soon grown old, their suffering renders them nearly unhuman in appearance. News film of them is strangely surreal. "Where is justice?" we cry.

Yet God's servant, the Christ, suffered even more.

He bore the wrath of God for the sin of the whole world. The thunder roared, the lightning struck the tree, and in burning blazing agony the light of life went out. The charred remains were gathered and placed in a borrowed tomb. The vengeance of God's wrath upon sin had fallen.

Remember, Isaiah wrote of the suffering servant that his "appearance was disfigured beyond that of any man and his form marred beyond human likeness" (52:14). So pummeled and punished, beaten and bruised, was Jesus that at his death he no longer looked human. Imagine it, and shudder as you do. The solidity of his bone and tissue had been crushed with the fierceness with which a log is first pulverized, then mashed and ground to pulp. He hung from the cross limp, skin sagging and swelling, organs internally bleeding, the victim of a murder so grotesque that nothing we'd read in any tabloid could equal it in horror. Beside that, and even worse for him, were the moments in his demise when he took our sin on his battered shoulders; Jesus the Son was completely severed from the fellowship of the Father. "Eli, Eli, lama sabachthani? . . . My God, My God, Why hast Thou forsaken Me?" came his mournful cry just before death (Matthew 27:46 NASB). In excruciating loneliness the Son gave up his life for your sin and mine. Yes, his exaltation is coming, but oh, the suffering he endured beforehand.

His authority. Christ's destiny involves suffering, exaltation, and finally, according to Isaiah, authority. In the prophet's words, "So also will he sprinkle many nations, and kings will shut their mouths because of him. For what they were not told, they will see, and what they have not heard, they will understand" (52:15 NIV).

What is meant by the phrase, Christ will "sprinkle the nations"? The Hebrew word used for "sprinkle" is a levitical term. It is the same word used for the sprinkling of blood for the cleansing of sin in the levitical or priestly system followed by the Jews (see Leviticus 16:14-19; 17:6). First John 2:2 tells us that Christ "is the atoning sacrifice for our sins, and not only for ours but also for the sins of the whole world" (NIV). Tying that together with Isaiah 52, we realize that Jesus actually "sprinkles" the entire world with his blood. His death served as an atoning sacrifice to cleanse us of our sin, to pay the penalty of our sin, to provide a means of redemption for the entire world. Anyone may come to Jesus in faith. It's that simple.

Who would have thought that a holy God would become man and in total humiliation pay the price required to compensate for our sin, our broken law? Surely not even kings, Isaiah exclaims, could conceive of it. Why, even monarchs will shut their mouths as they begin to understand the amazing love and matchless wisdom of the Lord. Thinking of it makes you want to break into a song of praise, doesn't it? We should be singing with Charles Wesley:

> And can it be that I should gain
> An interest in the Saviour's blood?
> Died He for me, who caused His pain?
> For me, who Him to death pursued?
> Amazing love! How can it be
> That Thou, my God, shouldst die for me?

In no place in scripture do we see God's wisdom made more obvious and compelling than in the death of Christ for sinners. No other sacrifice could have sufficed. No other means would have made it possible for us to be redeemed. On this note of triumph, Isaiah concluded his brief introduction to chapter 53 of his book. We've been treated to a preview; let's read on for the rest of the story.

The Career of the Servant—Isaiah 53:1-3

> Who has believed our message
>   and to whom has the arm of the Lord been revealed?
> He grew up before him like a tender shoot,
>   and like a root out of dry ground.
> He had no beauty or majesty to attract us to him,
>   nothing in his appearance that we should desire him.
> He was despised and rejected by men,
>   a man of sorrows, and familiar with suffering.
> Like one from whom men hide their faces
>   he was despised, and we esteemed him not
> (Isaiah 53:1-3 NIV).

I've titled this section "The Career of the Servant," and Christ's earthly mission is essentially what Isaiah described at the beginning of chapter 53. The prophet started by voicing two questions—actually laments. "Who has believed our message?" he despondently asked initially. It is a question originating with God.

Who has believed God's message? That's easy to answer: not many. Throughout the centuries few have been willing to acknowledge that only through the death and resurrection of Jesus is salvation possible. "But the natural man receiveth not the things of the Spirit of God: for they are foolishness unto him" (1 Corinthians 2:14 KJV; see also Matthew 7:13-14). God doesn't want it that way. Blinded eyes and unreceptive hearts grieve him greatly. He desires that all come to Christ in faith. In the words of the apostle Peter, "The Lord is not slow about His promise, as some count slowness, but is patient toward you, not wishing for any to perish but for all to come to repentance" (2 Peter 3:9 NASB).

Yet God leaves the choice up to us. He'll never violate our free will. He longs for glory from the obedient heart content to take him as he is. The tragic statistic is that most people, Jew and gentile alike, never respond to him *his* way. They go to the grave without ever coming into a relationship with Christ. They figure they're good enough to get to heaven on their own. They believe in God, after all. Why is this Christ stuff so important? There probably isn't a hell anyway, or if there is, it's the place for the Hitlers and the Stalins, for serial killers and racketeers, extortionists and terrorists.

Who believes God's message? Not even the people he has singled out, not even his chosen race, the descendants of Abraham. As a nation, the Jews still reject the offered messiah. The tragic truth remains: "He came unto his own, and his own received him not" (John 1:11 KJV).

> Hear, O heavens! Listen, O earth!
> For the Lord has spoken:
> "I reared children and brought them up,
> but they have rebelled against me.
> The ox knows his master,
> the donkey his owner's manger,
> but Israel does not know,
> my people do not understand"
> (Isaiah 1:2-3 NIV).

But some do understand. Some comprehend. Some hearts are softened by the water of the word. Wisdom prevails and eyes open to behold his glory. Voices are raised with that of the sightless man healed by Christ in John 9: Once I was blind, but now I see.

"To whom has the arm of the Lord been revealed?" Isaiah continued, voicing the second of his questions in 53:1. His words suggest a picture of a sleeve rolled up and an arm ready for action, prepared to go to work. What was God's greatest work? Was it the creation of the universe? No. The Lord merely spoke a syllable or two, and the world came into being (see Genesis 1). The heavens are "the work of thy fingers" says the psalmist in praise to the Lord (see Psalm 8:3 KJV).

It cost God far more to send his Son to the cross than it did to engineer the entire creation. The cross involved the total commitment of Jehovah to purchase our redemption. The cross was his greatest undertaking. And so, to whom is the Lord's arm revealed? The answer is, to those of us who accept his salvation and become new creations in Christ. God has rolled up his sleeves, wiped his brow, and lifted our load for us. We are the beneficiaries of his labor of love.

How did it all come about? God's servant, the Christ, didn't come blazing onto the scene astride a fireball from heaven. His spaceship did not land in some strategic spot to stake claim on a planet he had created. His entry into our world did not violate the laws of nature, except that his conception was miraculous. He was born in a manger. He "grew up . . . like a tender shoot" (Isaiah 53:2), and progressed through the normal stages of infancy and childhood. At twelve he startled the theologians in the temple in Jerusalem with his insights into his Father's word. After that episode, Luke 2:52 tells us that "Jesus kept increasing in wisdom and stature, and in favor with God and men" (NASB). He reached his thirties and began his public ministry. Three years later he made a sacrifice of himself on the brow of Golgotha.

Isaiah also said of the career of this "tender shoot," this servant/savior, that he grew "like a root out of dry ground" (53:2). Just as God had revealed in his word, among Christ's earthly ancestors were King David and David's father Jesse (see Matthew 1). In the last chapter we referred to the promise God made to David that an eternal heir would sit on David's throne, and that David's kingdom would be established forever (see 2 Samuel 7:12-16). Elsewhere Isaiah described Jesus as a "shoot" that "will come up from the stump of Jesse," a "Branch" that "will bear fruit" (Isaiah 11:1 NIV).

When Jesus walked the earth, there was no davidic king

sitting on the throne of Israel. Control of the government fell under the jurisdiction of the Roman empire. That Jesus' earthly lineage was one of Hebrew royalty made no difference to anybody. Given the circumstances, his credentials weren't the least bit impressive, his externals nothing to get excited about. In the words of the prophet, "He had no beauty or majesty to attract us to him, nothing in his appearance that we should desire him" (Isaiah 53:2 NIV). Do you realize that, were Jesus applying for the job of messiah, king of Israel, savior of his people, we probably wouldn't have hired him? The pastoral search committee would never have called him. We'd have turned him away. "Don't call us; we'll call you," we'd have said while tossing his resume into the circular file.

Thank God that his thoughts are not our thoughts, his ways are not ours. Things that impress us in our misguided humanity are often abominations to the Lord. The prophet Samuel had to learn that the hard way. When King Saul, a handsome man, towering head and shoulders above the rest, washed out royally and Samuel searched for God's appointed successor, the Lord instructed the prophet, "Do not consider his appearance or his height. . . . The Lord does not look at the things man looks at. Man looks at the outward appearance, but the Lord looks at the heart" (1 Samuel 16:7 NIV). Who was God's man for the job? None other than the youngest of Jesse's boys, David, a good-looking lad so green that no one even thought about his entering the competition, much less being in contention for the crown.

Christ came in a normal human body, just like everybody else. He couldn't have modeled in catalogs. He'd have sold no pin-up posters; he'd have inspired no games, toys, or made-for-TV movies; he'd have been offered no commercial endorsements. Throughout his public career he was "despised and rejected by men" (Isaiah 53:3). He was "a man of sorrows, and familiar with suffering. Like one from whom men hide their faces he was despised, and we esteemed him not" (53:3b-4).

The Lord came in flesh, and his flesh was despised. Humankind hated him. "Get rid of him!" we shouted. We nailed him to a wooden instrument of scorn, slaying his body through a method of execution so degrading that Roman citizens condemned to death were exempted from it, no matter how heinous their crimes. We plucked his beard, beat his body, bruised his head, pierced his side, and broke his heart. No, we weren't at Calvary, but our sins were. Each of us is able to cry, "O God in heaven, the guilt is mine; I crucified your Son divine!" We, with our inclination to sin, the sin nature we inherited from grandfather Adam, caused Christ to be on the cross. Our disobediences destroyed him. Still, so many of us fail to esteem him. We deny his divinity. We negate his sacrifice as we refuse to acknowledge his salvation. We ignore his sufferings. We hide our faces from the Son.

Even if we are Christians, having accepted his sacrifice by faith, we may still fail to esteem him properly. Do we easily admit we know him? No. Do we honestly admit we love him? No.

Get the picture? The real tragedy of Calvary was not the death of Jesus; therein also lay the victory. The real tragedy is that so many miss it, and even finding it, never truly value it.

The Suffering of the Servant—Isaiah 53:4-6

Surely he took up our infirmities
 and carried our sorrows,
yet we considered him stricken by God,
 smitten by him, and afflicted.
But he was pierced for our transgressions,
 he was crushed for our iniquities;
the punishment that brought us peace was upon him,
 and by his wounds we are healed.
We all, like sheep, have gone astray,
 each of us has turned to his own way;
and the Lord has laid on him
 the iniquity of us all.

One part of the cross which Isaiah didn't want to be forgotten is the suffering of the servant. We can't afford to forget it. Doing so makes us grow complacent about Calvary and discount the cross. In the midst of our own trials and troubles, we mustn't forget that our savior suffered all the more. Isaiah had already described in disturbing detail the death of the Son, yet he continued. His words had another purpose as well. They give us a glimpse into the mind of God, clarifying why Calvary had to be, describing how it all fits together in the Lord's plan to forgive us.

"Surely he took up our infirmities and carried our sorrows, yet we considered him stricken by God, smitten by him, and afflicted," wrote the prophet (53:4 NIV). In Leviticus 16 the Lord spelled out what was required of Aaron, the first Jewish high priest, in making atonement for the sins of the people:

> When Aaron has finished making atonement for the Most Holy Place, the Tent of Meeting and the altar, he shall bring forward the live goat. He is to lay both hands on the head of the live goat and confess over it all the wickedness and rebellion of the Israelites—all their sins—and put them on the goat's head. He shall send the goat away into the desert in the care of a man appointed for the task. The goat will carry on itself all their sins to a solitary place; and the man shall release it in the desert (Leviticus 16:20-22 NIV).

It was God's plan from the very beginning, from the garden of Eden until the end of time as we know it, that Jesus Christ would become our scapegoat. Like the sacrificial animal mentioned in Leviticus, he would carry our sins to a solitary place, a place of separation from God the Father. He would pay the price of our disobedience once for all time.

Think of the burden involved as he bore our sins. Think of God searching for a way to forgive us. Think of God himself willing to carry us.

I'm reminded of an incident that happened to me in St. John a few years ago. One of the things I look forward to with excitement about going to Canada, besides getting to minister to the terrific folks there, is a chance to spend some time on the Atlantic coast. That particular year the weather was quite severe. New-fallen snow covered everything. Fifty to sixty miles-per-hour winds and blowing snow made seaside excursions impractical, to say the least. The end of the conference week approached, and the climate hadn't cooperated sufficiently for us to visit the shore. I was disappointed, but then a couple of hearty souls who wanted me to have a chance to pick up some rocks and shells, and see how lobsters were caught and scallops captured, volunteered to drive me to the beach in their pickup.

While we were heading for the coast, my friends, a father and son, informed me that we were going to come to the place where the tides flow greater than anywhere else in the world. We're not talking about six- or eight-foot-high walls of water, but tides of thirty-four feet or more at their highest. When we finally reached seaside, it was cold. Even at the coast, snow blanketed everything except the rocky beach. The wind blew fiercely as I waddled out of the cab of the pickup, bundled up in two enormous Arctic parkas like an overstuffed teddy bear.

We set out for a walk on the beach. The tide was out quite a way, so we ambled across the damp stones of a little inlet. Like a kid at Disneyland, I became lost in wonder, scrambling awkwardly on rocks, finding periwinkles, and stuffing shells and pebbles into my pockets. My friends indulged me with good humor. I don't know how long we spent on the other side of that inlet, but when we started back for the truck, we saw that there had been a change. The tide had begun to come in, and instead of walking across the inlet rocks, we were going to have to wade through three feet of water. Snow pelted us; the wind-driven blasts were more fierce than any I'd ever encountered. The thought of sloshing through pools of icy water was not appealing. Besides, I'd have to unload the precious cargo of shells and stones bulging in my pockets. Seeing my concern, Hilton, the son, a strapping young fellow, spoke up.

"Don, don't worry about it. I'm going to carry you over."

"Hilton, you've got to be kidding!" I replied. "I'm two times your size with all this padding. Besides, my pockets are full of rocks."

Before I could argue further, he pulled off his shoes and socks, rolled up his pants, and strode quickly through the deep water. He laid his dry boots and socks safely on the other side, then waded back across. With a grunt and a groan, he hoisted me on his back, a bulging burden with legs tightly wrapped around his waist. Then he carted me, rocks and all, across the inlet, gently setting me down on the other side. He grabbed his boots and sped in his bare feet to the cab of the pickup, where he started the engine and turned on the heater full blast.

"I can't believe you did that!" I exclaimed when we'd all safely climbed back into the truck.

"It would've been easier if you hadn't had all those rocks," Hilton commented with a grin.

How unselfishly and lovingly that young man met my needs. He went far beyond the call of duty to assist me. He greatly inconvenienced himself just to keep me dry and comfortable. I thought about Isaiah 53:4. I was a burden that my willing helper, Hilton, was happy to bear. So are we believers to God. The Lord will bear us where we cannot walk. He'll take us through the stormy Jordan and set us down gently on the other side. Why? Because he loves us unconditionally.

Do you realize that God actually had to search for a way to forgive us? Think about it. When someone does you wrong—talks about you behind your back, cheats you out of some money, lies about you, insults your spouse or children, reneges on an obligation—how easy is it for you to forgive the wrongdoer? Maybe if he or she is lucky, you'll forgive them. But it'll take time. And it sure helps if they ask for forgiveness first, and make appropriate apologies and restitution. But God didn't see things that way. He didn't wait around for us to make the first move. He sent his Son to the cross. And there, as was prophesied some seven hundred years before it happened, the Lord Jesus "was pierced for our transgressions, . . . crushed for our iniquities; the punishment that brought us peace was upon him, and by his wounds we are healed" (Isaiah 53:5 NIV). The thunder of Sinai, the flashing of the lightning across a darkened sky, and the judgment of God came pouring down on our substitute, our savior. Despised, forsaken, he wrestled in an anguish we cannot comprehend, to give us a victory we do not deserve.

Wait a minute, you say. I'm a pretty decent person. I give to the United Way. I don't abuse alchohol or drugs. I don't cheat on my income taxes or on my wife. I play with my kids. I put food on the table and a roof over my family's head. I'm a nice guy. Why did Jesus have to die for me? Why can't the good things in my life outweigh the bad? Surely the scales are tipped in my favor. C'mon!

When that's our mind-set, it's because we've failed to reckon with the mind of God. Isaiah 64:6 says that all our deeds of righteousness are as "filthy rags" to our Father in heaven. What we do on our own, apart from Jesus Christ, amounts to nothing in the eyes of God. "We all, like sheep, have gone astray, each of us has turned to his own way; and the Lord has laid on him the iniquity of us all," Isaiah wrote (53:6 NIV). The purpose of Jesus' suffering was to take our punishment. God's standard is perfection, and we can't be good enough on our own to get to heaven. There will always be something, some dishonorable desire, some action or thought, to keep us from hitting God's flawless mark. Isaiah says that we *all* like sheep have gone astray. Not a one of us of our own volition has opted to stay in the flock, or been able to remain totally obedient to the Lord. Here are some other verses that ought to convince us that, by ourselves, the picture isn't too pretty:

All have turned away,
 they have together become worthless;
there is no one who does good,
 not even one (Romans 3:12 NIV).

For all have sinned and fall short of the glory of God
 (Romans 3:23 NIV).

Surely I was sinful at birth,
 sinful from the time my mother conceived me
 (Psalm 51:5 NIV).

The heart is deceitful above all things
 and beyond cure.
 Who can understand it? (Jeremiah 17:9 NIV).

Sir Winston Churchill, commending the valor of the RAF during World War II, said, "Never have so many owed so much to so few." Backdating it to Calvary, we can say that never have we all owed so much to one.

The Obedience of the Servant—Isaiah 53:7-9

He was oppressed and afflicted,
 yet he did not open his mouth;
he was led like a lamb to the slaughter,
 and as a sheep before her shearers is silent,
 so he did not open his mouth.
By oppression and judgment, he was taken away.
 And who can speak of his descendants?
For he was cut off from the land of the living;
 for the transgression of my people he was stricken.
He was assigned a grave with the wicked,
 and with the rich in his death,
though he had done no violence,
 nor was any deceit in his mouth (NIV).

How ironic, that the guilty should be punished, yet we can be set free. The innocent suffers and dies in our stead. Our hearts democratically cry, "Not fair!" And yet we must thank God that in allowing Christ to die he wasn't being humanly fair, but infinitely kind. He was doing what he had already said he would do in the prophetic word.

The events of Easter week fulfilled biblical prophecy to the letter as did the entire life of Jesus. In the last chapter we discussed how Christ's triumphal Palm Sunday entry into Jerusalem to present himself to his people was foretold in Zechariah 9:9. Each detail of his human existence fulfilled the hundreds of biblical prophecies that specifically concerned his life, death, and resurrection. In Isaiah 53 we see a few of them.

"He was oppressed and afflicted, yet he did not open his mouth; he was led like a lamb to the slaughter, and as a sheep before her shearers is silent, so he did not open his mouth," wrote the prophet (53:7 NIV). In the New Testament we read its fulfillment. When Jesus was dragged before Pilate, he refused to open his mouth in self-defense. He uttered no words of explanation. He said nothing, so that even Pilate was amazed (Matthew 27:12-19).

How different Christ was in his silence than we probably would be. Think about it. When you're offended, do you keep your mouth shut, or do you tell whoever will listen? Do you keep quiet when somebody slights you or cheats you? Probably not. It's acceptable in our society to pop off in reply. "You'll hear from my attorney!" we're quick to threaten. We feel we've got to stand up for our rights. We've somehow, in our culture, adopted the idea that silent submission is not a quality of great men but of Casper Milquetoasts. Even the so-called strong, silent types—the John Waynes, the Clint Eastwoods—stoically plot their revenge while they're being wronged. We equate acceptance and meekness with weakness, and it just isn't so. Christ was no coward, quivering before his accusers. Keeping one's mouth clamped in the hour of pressure is the height of strength. Christ's silence was a sign of his power and control.

I wouldn't have been silent in his place, would you? Knowing Old Testament prophecy as he did, knowing what torment lay ahead? Knowing what pain he'd suffer? I would have pleaded my case, called the angels from the heavens to protect me. At the very least, I would have reminded the soldiers who I was and whose I was. I'd have argued with the Jewish leaders about the meaning of Isaiah 53. "Listen, fellows, you're making a BIG mistake," I'd have insisted. Were I the Lord, the inventor of languages, every vocabulary word in the universe would have been at my command. I'd have launched a counterplot, bribed some guards, called down fire from heaven. I'd have blown out the sun, called for a flood, covered the world with frogs and locusts—anything to avoid the cross.

But Jesus didn't indulge in fast talking.

Jesus didn't say a word.

They spit at him, mocked him, dragged him across the pavement, laughed at his weakness. But he kept his peace. Still he held his tongue. Why wouldn't he fight and defend himself?

Even Terry Fox, a hero if ever there was one, once cried *foul* against a columnist who'd printed inaccuracies about his run of hope. The negative hype got to Terry. In tears he hung up the phone after speaking to the newsman, and in frustration considered throwing in the towel. It seemed people didn't really care, and that discouraged him.

Jesus didn't throw in the towel. There's no indication in scripture that he even considered such action. And he was God of the universe, the one individual with a right to be frustrated by the flawed responses of his children.

The God of the universe was "by oppression and judgment . . . taken away. . . . cut off from the land of the living; for the transgression of my people he was stricken" (Isaiah 53:8 NIV). God the Son died on the cross. Every gospel records it. He could have hollered, "Stop! I want to get off! I quit! They don't care anyway!" But instead he saw it through to the end, hanging in for the finish and thus paving a way for a new beginning for us.

In the end, he "was assigned a grave with the wicked" (Isaiah 53:9 NIV). Christ the messiah should have been buried with executed criminals. He should have been tossed into a common burial ground, a pauper's grave, laid to rest with the guilty elements who died on crosses. But Jesus was "with the rich in his death," as the prophet predicted (Isaiah 53:9 NIV).

Matthew 27:57-60 tells us that Joseph of Arimathea, a wealthy man and secret follower of Christ, took the Lord's body and placed it in his family crypt. In this way the prophecy was fulfilled. Only the very rich had such tombs, and so with the wealthiest of men the martyred Jesus lay.

These are only a smattering of the Old Testament prophecies fulfilled precisely in Christ Jesus. They all came true. And somehow the Jewish leaders of the day missed it, completely.

The Reward of the Servant—Isaiah 53:10-12

> Yet it was the Lord's will to crush him and cause him to suffer,
> and though the Lord makes his life a guilt offering,
> he will see his offspring and prolong his days,
> and the will of the Lord will prosper in his hand.
> After the suffering of his soul,
> he will see the light of life and be satisfied;
> by his knowledge my righteous servant will justify many,
> and he will bear their iniquities.
> Therefore I will give him a portion among the great,
> and he will divide the spoils with the strong,
> because he poured out his life unto death,
> and was numbered with the transgressors.
> For he bore the sin of many,
> and made intercession for the transgressors (NIV).

Isaiah pointed out next that it was the Lord's will to crush the Christ. My personal translation of the Hebrew text suggests that Isaiah 53:10 might even read, "Jehovah was pleased to crush him." Why? Why could God be happy to have Jesus killed? Why was he pleased to allow his servant to suffer? It's because God preferred that his Son die rather than that sin prevail. He hated sin so much that he crushed his Son, because that was the final solution.

And the Son got a chance to view the results of his sacrifice. Isaiah 53:11 is God speaking directly; it contains a promise that after the suffering of his soul, the messiah will see the light of life and be satisfied. There is light at the end of the tunnel. Jesus didn't just die and stay in the darkness of the grave. He rose again! Now people can respond to his sacrifice. He faced down our opposition; now we have opportunity. First came his affliction and it all worked to our advantage. Hebrews 12:2 calls Christ "the author and perfecter of faith, who for the joy set before Him endured the cross, despising the shame, and has sat down at the right hand of the throne of God" (NASB). Through the storm to the calm, through the trial to the triumph, through the shame to the honor—so went the savior.

The result? "By his knowledge my righteous servant will justify many." That's what happens with every believer. Christ justifies him or her. Justification means making us "just as if" we'd never sinned, and that is what Jesus does. He washes our slates clean. He declares us righteous in his sight. We're totally acceptable, cleansed of the leprosy of sin, standing in the company of the redeemed, washed by the blood of the lamb.

Isaiah summed it all up in 53:12, where we read that the servant, Christ:

1. "Poured out his life unto death"—actually physically died on the cross
2. "Was numbered with the transgressors"—became identified with sinners, although he was sinless

3. "Bore the sin of many"—became our sin-bearer
4. "Made intercession for the transgressors"—now is our intercessor at the right hand of the Father (see also Hebrews 1:3).

The Bridge of Life

Jesus is the bridge connecting us to the Father. He's interceding for us right now. Even as you're reading this, he is pleading your case. Under the levitical system of atonement, the priests' work was never done. There were no chairs in the tabernacle or the temple. Now there is no longer a need for smoking altars, dying lambs, and human priestly intercessors. Jesus Christ, God's Son, put an end to all of that. As Paul wrote to Timothy, "For there is one God, and one mediator also between God and men, the man Christ Jesus" (1 Timothy 2:5 NASB). The writer of the book of Hebrews put it this way:

> Hence, also, He is able to save forever those who draw near to God through Him, since He always lives to make intercession for them.
>
> For it was fitting that we should have such a high priest, holy, innocent, undefiled, separated from sinners and exalted above the heavens; who does not need daily, like those high priests, to offer up sacrifices, first for His own sins, and then for the sins of the people, because this He did once for all when He offered Himself (Hebrews 7:25-27; see also Hebrews 4:14-16; 10:12,19-22).

Jesus Christ waits today to meet your needs. The greatest of these needs is that of salvation. If you think you're okay because you're a relatively moral person, you're wrong. Scripturally, none of us is righteous. God's standards for entry into heaven and fellowship with him are too high. None of us can attain them. If we've thought even one bad thought, we've failed. The stopwatch has stopped before the race has started.

The answer is Calvary. Atonement has been provided at the cross. The high priestly sacrifice has been made there, once for all time. It will never be exhausted. As Alexander Whyte wrote, "After that fountain filled with blood has drowned in the depths of the sea all the accusations that my sinful life has raised against me, that same blood will still flow for you and will do the same service for you. And the blood of Christ is the same blood yesterday, today, and for ever."

The blood of Christ. Yesterday, today, and forever. This Easter, think of it. And with William Cowper, raise your voice in praise and thanksgiving that:

> There is a fountain filled with blood
> Drawn from Immanuel's veins;
> And sinners, plunged beneath that flood,
> Lose all their guilty stains.

Thank God, this Easter, we can be whiter than snow.

Reflections for the season

1. What human heroes do you especially admire? Do their sacrifices even begin to equal that of Jesus Christ?

2. These days we are often attracted to celebrities. Many covet the lifestyles of the rich and famous. We are drawn to beauty, wealth, sophistication, trendiness. Reread Isaiah 53. Did Jesus Christ fit the stereotype of the "rich and famous"? Would his face be splashed across magazine covers and society pages? What can we learn about our own priorities from Isaiah's description of Christ?

3. In your opinion, is the real tragedy of Calvary the fact that Jesus died there? Why or why not?

C H A P T E R F O U R

The Psalm of the Cross

Psalm 22

Crosses. Gilded ones are suspended from sanctuary ceilings, golden ones dangle from chains around our necks, silver ones with ribbons attached slide into our Bibles to mark pages, carved ones adorn plaques, paperweights, and picture frames. Jewelers stock them by the score come spring; they compete with Bibles as the bestsellers of the Easter season. For some of us, crosses proclaim our Christianity; for others, the symbol serves only as an accessory. We wear them—and we also bear them.

"Oh, what an insufferable cross I have to bear!" a sanctimonious character in a play complains about his addled wife. The often-repeated statement lends comic relief to the plot, but the serious reality is that we don't just wear crosses as jewelry; we're often called to bear incredibly heavy, harsh ones as we plug along through life. Christians are by no means immune to suffering. We journey over our own way of suffering, just as Jesus did centuries ago. Our enemies are Pilates, Pharisees, and Roman soldiers of different sorts: diseases, depression, death—the diverse disasters of body, soul, mind, and spirit. What follows is the story of an agonizing cross borne this side of Calvary, the account of two friends of our ministry who've regularly attended our Bible classes in the central Texas city they call home.

Bearing the Cross

It all finally made sense to Jean one day. She'd attended church most of her life, been involved in youth activities and Sunday school. She'd married a young Christian man. They'd settled down to raise a family, found a good church, become involved in the community. But there was still an emptiness inside her, something she didn't understand. She tried hard to be a good person, to do the right things, to keep herself calm with the kids, to stay cheerful around her husband, family, and friends. But she didn't feel complete. She felt frustrated, guilty, depressed, sometimes even angry.

Then one day it happened.

What she'd been hearing about in church finally jelled into a cohesive whole. A light dawned and she sank to her knees in amazed gratitude and asked Jesus Christ to be her savior. Relief and release washed over her, and for the first time in her life this young mother felt complete.

In succeeding years, Jean was a changed person. Her Christian activities were different—she didn't teach Sunday school or volunteer for jobs because she felt she had to, but because she wanted to out of love for the Lord. Each of her three children received Christ as savior. As years passed and the children grew up and left home one by one, Jean found employment as an executive secretary at a large corporation. She was warm, friendly, funny, vibrant in her faith, articulate in speech and writing. She traveled; she loved to try new things. Photographs of a trip to Israel show her laughing as she gamely sat atop a camel. Even after her own kids left home, she stayed involved with the young, leading Bible studies for teenaged girls in her home. These "girl talk" sessions are fond memories for many even today, some eight years after the last one.

During those years, Jean also worked in a local prison ministry. Saturday afternoons were times to travel to the city jail and meet with prisoners for services, sharing the gospel with them. Prostitutes, drug traffickers, thieves, and con artists were among those whom she counseled. "You're different," said the wife of a notorious mob hit man in custody as an accessory to her husband's latest crime, the assassination of a federal judge. Touched by Jean's unaffected warmth and kindness, she said, "I like you."

Jean viewed the idea of turning fifty with considerably better humor than most women. Her youngest child was in college, the middle one soon to be married, the oldest well established on his own, with a wife, home, and career. So fifty was no problem. The kids were okay. She and her husband Gerry wouldn't have too many years till retirement, and were actually looking forward to the empty nest. Her kids gave her a fiftieth birthday party with friends and family. It was a day to remember.

Not long afterward would come other days never to be forgotten. It came about subtly, insidiously. First there were slight lapses of memory and episodes of confusion. Jean would be driving down the road and for a few panic-filled moments would forget where she was and where she was going. Work became tough, then impossible. The telephones with their flashing lights and loud buzzing, which she had once handled so deftly, now bewildered her. She'd press the wrong button, lift the receiver incorrectly, cut off the caller. Her once-firm handwriting became shaky and difficult to read. Messages were garbled. It happened slowly, almost imperceptibly. But it became obvious that she had trouble doing the job, and when a corporate restructuring mandated massive layoffs, she was among those to be let go.

The next few years were both marked by joy and tainted with tragedy. Happy events took place in the family: college graduations, marriages, the births of grandchildren. Jean enjoyed the good times, but with each passing month her confusion increased and her inability to communicate grew worse. A thick fog descended, and Jean became less and less capable. She ironed shirts to help one daughter-in-law following the birth of a grandchild. Four years later, she was unable even to hold the newest grandbabies without assistance. Dressing herself became impossible; eating was a chore. Two of her favorite pastimes, writing and reading, had long proved too difficult. Now, as I write these words, even watching television is an exercise in futility for her.

Doctors? Yes, eleven have been consulted. Tests have been run by the score: blood work, batteries of neurological evaluations, catscans, EEGs, MRIs—medically, it's all been done. The diagnosis isn't certain, but diseases like Alzheimer's have no cure.

Today, still in her fifties, Jean looks forward to holidays, Sundays at church, times with the family. She isn't sure when anything is going to happen; tomorrow is the same as next month to her, in her concept of time and space. Daily her husband helps her dress, applies her make-up, prepares her meals, and reassures her when the fog becomes nightmarish. Her children and parents, family and friends, come to visit and help however they can; they take her out when she's able. She still smiles and recognizes others and inquires about those she loves. But life isn't what anyone thought it would be for her. It isn't what anyone hoped it would be—not her husband, her kids, her grandchildren who won't truly know her, her mom and dad who approach their eighties heartsick at her deterioration. God can cure her. He may well do so. Or she may never be whole again until she is directly in his presence. There she'll receive a many-jeweled crown for what she's endured. And beside her at some point with equal reward will be the man she married, one who loves her with all his breaking heart, and who sacrificially, unselfishly, tenderly, serves her, giving his children the priceless privilege of witnessing true commitment in action.

"I just don't understand it. She's such a sweet person, such a wonderful Christian. She's done so much for the Lord." I hear those comments all the time about Jean's condition. The family hears them too. And they also wonder why.

It doesn't seem fair, does it? Human tragedy never does. Suffering leaves a bitter taste in our mouths. The futility of an apparently wasted life frustrates us, enrages us, makes us rail at the reality of our own lack of control, our impotence to change circumstances. "God, it just isn't right!" we cry in desperation. "Why did you let this happen? How could you?" And we blame him. Yet there is a twofold perspective we must not forget, even in the midst of our fury, hurt, and tears.

From Our Father's Eyes

At the funeral of a two-year-old boy at which I helped to officiate, another minister began his address to the congregation with these words, "God isn't fair." Hey, I thought, we don't need to hear that. What do you think you're doing? Skeptically I continued to listen—and soon appreciated the enormous wisdom of his words.

"God isn't fair," said the minister, "but God is always kind." What he meant was this. Things that happen to us, particularly tough things like the loss of a child or the onset of illness, may not seem fair from our limited human perspective. But from the vantage point of eternity they all fit together somehow. In the midst of the valley of the shadow, the Lord is infinitely kind. What hits us in this life passes by him first; each tragedy and triumph is Father-filtered, sifted through his omnipotent hands, screened by his omniscient consciousness.

To us, it isn't fair that a two-year-old dies.

It isn't fair that a couple desperately longing for children proves infertile.

It isn't fair that a young father on the battlefield sacrifices his limbs and ability to earn a livelihood.

It isn't fair that a vibrant middle-aged woman loses the capacity to function normally.

It isn't fair that doctors misdiagnose, drunk drivers hit and run, chemotherapy treatments fail, vision and hearing are lost.

It isn't fair, but somehow, some way, it is still kind.

You're not convinced? It's because you're not God. You can't see with his eyes, think with his mind, hear with his ears, feel with his emotions. You don't, and perhaps won't, know the *whys* behind the *whats* until you reach eternity. What's left? It can only be that we've got to trust him in the trials. That's all we can do.

As a young woman, Jean committed herself to Jesus Christ. She'd be the first to tell you, could she still communicate clearly, that the Lord loves her. She'd be the first to acknowledge his wisdom in allowing what has happened. She'd be the first to verbalize her trust.

Why should we trust him? There are countless reasons why he is worthy of it and two reasons stand out for me especially.

First, there is eternity to consider. The heartaches and hassles of human life are temporary. "For momentary, light affliction is producing for us an eternal weight of glory far beyond all comparison" (2 Corinthians 4:17 NASB), wrote the apostle Paul, who had certainly known his share of physical, mental, and emotional suffering. Paul wrote specifically of the tough times he endured in 2 Corinthians 11:24-28:

> Five times I received from the Jews thirty-nine lashes. Three times I was beaten with rods, once I was stoned, three times I was shipwrecked, a night and a day I have spent in the deep. I have been on frequent journeys, in dangers from rivers, dangers from robbers, dangers from my countrymen, dangers from the Gentiles, dangers in the city, dangers in the wilderness, dangers on the sea, dangers among false brethren; I have been in labor and hardship, through many sleepless nights, in hunger and thirst, often without food, in cold and exposure. Apart from such external things, there is the daily pressure upon me of concern for all the churches (NASB; see also 2 Corinthians 4:8-10).

Whew! Reading that discourse of distress makes my personal disasters seem less devastating. What about you? Paul also tells us in Philippians 1:29 that for Christians "it has been granted for Christ's sake, not only to believe in Him, but also to suffer for His sake" (NASB). We're actually supposed to expect the test. We believers should anticipate trouble as we trudge through human life. And it's essential that when the darts are thrown our way, we keep God's outlook in view, arming ourselves with the shield of faith described in Ephesians 6:12.

To a God not bound by limits of time and space, our lives are but eyeblinks in eternity. The temporal will one day be transformed into the everlasting, and if we know Christ as savior, we'll dwell eternally with the Lord in his house, surrounded by his glory. The idea of *forever* with him makes even decades of human hardship seem insignificant in comparison. We've got to grasp hold of the eternal perspective! Keeping our eyes on the ultimate helps us more effectively deal with the here and now. A man I know from East Texas maintains that right attitude. Reflecting on the loss of his two preschool-aged children years ago, he said, "I'm getting older now, and I'm getting ready. Soon I'm going to see my children, and I won't be coming back."

Nothing catches God by surprise so that he has to say, "Oh, I made a mistake. I missed on that one. I didn't realize it was going to turn out that way." He holds all our moments in his hand and gives them to us one by one. There are no mistakes. No thwarted purposes. No frustrated intentions. No news of a botched-up plan will ever greet us in glory. "For now we see in a mirror dimly, but then face to face; now I know in part, but then I shall know fully just as I also have been fully known" (1 Corinthians 13:12 NASB; see also 2:9). The God of the hereafter is also in charge of the here and now.

Second, we must trust in God's kindness because his Son has suffered immensely, unimaginably, himself. The Son endured human physical torment worse than any we'll face. He sustained mental anguish, suffered emotional upheaval. He knew loss, injury, rejection, betrayal. The writer to the Hebrews said this of what Christ experienced: "Since then the children share in flesh and blood, He Himself likewise also partook of the same, that through death He might render powerless him who had the power of death, that is, the devil" (Hebrews 2:14 NASB; see also 2:15-18). The Lord Jesus ran the gauntlet, fought the duel, scaled the summit, fell into the abyss. He experienced it all.

Because he has, we know he understands.
Because he did it, we know he cares.

A Psalm of the Suffering Savior

God's suffering is what we'll see as we turn to the second of our photographs of Calvary, Psalm 22. This time it's the cross from God's perspective that we witness. We'll feel we are there, our hands nailed to the boards, our limbs torn, our bodies bleeding. Psalm 22 is not for the light reader. It isn't sugar-coated poetry, but vivid, gut-wrenching verse. By looking at Isaiah 53, we've seen *why* God went to Calvary. Now we'll witness *what he did* there, in all its intensity. We'll know what it was like to hang on a cross. We'll hear the words of the savior as he sacrificed himself. We'll experience the hurt of a parent losing a beloved child. We'll know God's side of Calvary—even as Abraham knew when he offered up Isaac. It ought to break our hearts.

And hopefully we'll realize that no matter what the torment of this present life, there is an afterlife. Heaven is out there, and it's going to be wonderful. There is an eternal perspective worthy of our focus. Jesus said to the thief on the cross, "Today you will be with me in paradise," and that's good enough for me. We know a Christ who has passed through blood, tears, and death, and who loved us enough to endure it.

Who wrote Psalm 22? The author was David, the earthly ancestor of Jesus, the king to whom God promised an eternal kingdom and eternal heir (see 2 Samuel 7:16). A talented musician, David wrote most of the psalms (which are really songs) found in the Bible.

Why do we believe that Psalm 22 is about the messiah? Many of the psalms of David are actually prophecies concerning Christ, each fulfilled or yet to be fulfilled in him. They specifically address issues relating to the messiah's death, resurrection, and coming kingdom. Jesus said, "All things which are written about Me in the Law of Moses and the Prophets *and the Psalms* must be fulfilled" (Luke 24:44 NASB, italics mine). Still, it should be pointed out that some critics believe that the events described in Psalm 22 describe happenings in the life of David, not Jesus. Yet as we read it, I am confident you'll be convinced that this simply isn't so. It couldn't be. The picture so graphically painted is of an execution by crucifixion. Nothing in David's own earthly experience ever approached this brand of suffering. He could only have been recording what had been divinely revealed to him.

Among the miracles of the psalm is that it was written over one thousand years before the crucifixion of Christ took place. That form of execution was not even practiced in David's day. David knew nothing about the pain of dying on a cross, except what he saw in the glimpses of the future given him by the Holy Spirit. If you read this chapter and walk away unconvinced that David viewed a technicolor preview of the death of his greatest descendant, then I've failed to explain it adequately. Calvary is there in the text for all to see.

When reading Psalm 22 we should also take a look at Psalms 23 and 24, and I recommend you do so. The first gives us the cross; there we see Jesus as the good shepherd who gives his life for his sheep. Psalm 23 is the picture of Christ as the shepherd who cares for his sheep. Psalm 24 shows us Christ as the chief shepherd who one day comes for his sheep. It's the cross, the crook, and the crown that David foretells.

When he wrote of the promised seed back in Genesis 3:15, little did Moses know that the sacred thread of Jesus Christ would penetrate all of scripture and would wind around a rugged hill, there to find the cross where the Son of God would die. Little did David realize that his eternal heir was destined to suffer an excruciating physical death before experiencing glorious resurrection.

The first part of Psalm 22 (22:1-21) is a sob, a heartcry; the second portion (22:22-31) is a song of joy and coming glory. Many commentators believe that David's words there provided the inspiration for Christ's statements from the cross; some even suggest that Jesus may have repeated the psalm over and over again at Calvary. I'm convinced that the Lord had Psalm 22 in mind as he approached his death. From the cross, Jesus actually voiced the first statement of the psalm, the question, "My God, my God, why have you forsaken me?" (Psalm 22:1; see also Matthew 27:46). The last of David's words in Psalm 22 convey the same thoughts as the final words of Jesus as recorded by his friend John: "It is finished" (John 19:30).

I believe that Psalm 22 reveals to us the seven sayings of Jesus as he prepared to meet physical death. As we have noted, in some cases at Calvary, Christ directly quoted verses from the psalm. In other instances, the thoughts expressed by the tormented Jesus are the same as those recorded by David. Here's a brief outline to illustrate how Psalm 22 can be broken into sections and seen as the framework of Christ's final script:

I. Psalm 22:1-6: "My God, my God, why have you forsaken me?" (Matthew 27:46).

II. Psalm 22:7-8: "Father, forgive them for they do not know what they are doing" (Luke 23:34).

III. Psalm 22:9-11: "Woman, behold your son! . . . Behold your mother!" (John 19:26-27).

IV. Psalm 22:12-18: "I am thirsty" (John 19:28).

V. Psalm 22:19-21: "Father, into your hands I am committing my spirit" (Luke 23:46).

VI. Psalm 22:22-30: "Today you shall be with me in the Paradise" (Luke 23:43).
VII. Psalm 22:31: "It is finished" (John 19:30).

Surely Jesus had David's song in mind. The psalm catalogs his ordeal in intimate detail. Let's turn to the pages of scripture for a second snapshot of the savior at the cross he bore for us.

I. My God, My God, Why Have You Forsaken Me? Psalm 22:1-6

> My God, my God, why have you forsaken me?
> Why are you so far from saving me,
> so far from the words of my groaning?
> O my God, I cry out by day, but you do not answer,
> by night, and am not silent.
> Yet you are enthroned as the Holy One,
> you are the praise of Israel.
> In you our fathers put their trust;
> they trusted and you delivered them.
> They cried to you and were saved;
> in you they trusted and were not disappointed.
> But I am a worm and not a man,
> scorned by men and despised by the people (NIV).

The Loneliness of the Cross

"My God, my God, why have you forsaken me?" began David in Psalm 22:1. "Why are you so far from saving me, so far from the words of my groaning?" The three questions paint verbal portraits of loneliness. At approximately ten minutes till three on the afternoon of his death, Jesus himself said much the same thing. We read in Matthew 27:45-46:

> Now from the sixth hour darkness fell upon all the land until the ninth hour. And about the ninth hour Jesus

> cried out with a loud voice, saying, "Eli, Eli, Lama Sabachthani?" that is, "My God, my God, why hast thou forsaken Me?" (NASB).

The sheer desolation of complete isolation. Jesus knew all about it as he hung from the cross. Then, and only then, did he experience separation from his heavenly Father. Then, and only then, did the Father forsake him. Why? Why did the Father desert the Son at his moment of greatest need? Why did the groanings of the Lord fall on the deaf ears of God at the climax of Calvary? We cannot help but ask such questions when we read Christ's lament of loneliness. He knew what it was like to be homeless, friendless, and finally severed from the one enduring source of encouragement and strength, his heavenly Father.

Jesus knew he'd be alone at the end. He predicted it the night before in the upper room of a home where he had shared a last supper with his disciples. He told his closest friends about the coming events, and he warned that every man there would leave before the final curtain fell. They'd check out on him. They wouldn't hang around for the bitter end. Peter robustly argued, "No, we won't! We'll stick by you!" But a few hours later we find even self-confident Peter violently cursing and vehemently denying he'd ever known the Lord (see Matthew 26:31-35,69-75). The apostle John, Mary the mother of Jesus, and a few other women stood at the foot of the cross. But the rest were not around. They'd jumped ship. They'd scattered like termites into the woodwork. They'd gone while the going was good.

Yes, Christ knew he'd essentially be humanly alone at Calvary. And since he was all-knowing God, he knew that God the Father would have to desert him too. Separation from the Father was something he'd never known, a sensation he'd never experienced. The awful aloneness of an unsaved soul—he'd never encountered it. God was always there, his constant companion. When Christ's humanity made him tired from ministering to the multitudes, it was to the company of the Father that he'd withdraw. In the desert, on the mountaintops, in the garden of Gethsemane, he drew his strength from the limitless resources of heaven. The Father was with him in prison, surrounded him when he was scourged, sustained him when the nails were driven through his palms. But, for his final hours at the cross, his sacrifice had to be total. Christ had always counted on his Father. Now his Father turned his back.

Why? "He made Him who knew no sin to be sin on our behalf, that we might become the righteousness of God in Him" (2 Corinthians 5:21 NASB). "And He Himself bore our sins in His body on the cross, that we might die to sin and live to righteousness; for by His wounds you were healed" (1 Peter 2:24 NASB). For the three hours in which the darkness fell, at the time the Father withdrew his fellowship from the beloved Son, Jesus was being made sin for us. He was taking on his shoulders all the law's demands and human disobediences beginning in the garden of Eden. His cross was that of confrontation with sin. It was all laid on him. The courts of the earth declared him guilty and nailed him there. The courts of heaven looked on with Father-imposed impotence. The angels waited for a word from the Father to liberate the suffering Son, and heaven was silent. Such restraint in the midst of crisis is beyond our comprehension. God's redeeming grace—oh, how costly. What love! It was not that the Father loved the Son less, but that he hated sin more.

And so Jesus paid the price. All of it!

Jesus bore our sin. All of it!

Jesus died alone. The only one who qualified for the job. Nobody else *could* or *would.*

The Work of the Cross

"Why are you so far from saving me, so far from the words of my groaning?" David wrote, recording what must surely have been the thoughts of Christ at Calvary. Why would God not draw near to save him from some of the suffering, even an iota of the intense isolation? It's because salvation was to be the work of the Son. Our redemption was planned by the Father and purchased by the Son.

The Son had to suffer. He had to be separated from the Father in the midst of his agony, his groanings. In that way he showed us what obedience really is. It's when we suffer and hurt that humanly we resist, rebel, and long to run away. The supreme test of obedience comes when we really ache. Can we stay by the stuff, submit ourselves to what the Lord has allowed, and accept whatever comes, knowing that in his sovereign purpose God is molding it all for our good and growth, and for his glory? By permitting him to suffer, God the Father allowed God the Son to become our faithful high priest. Just as he suffered, we who are his children will suffer too. We probably won't hang from crosses, though perhaps Peter and others eventually did. But we'll know hardship. We'll be susceptible to the spectrum of human tragedy. Car accidents and plane crashes happen to Christians too. But we will be able to turn in prayer to a high priest, a Jesus Christ who's been there, who cares, who understands, who is able to sustain us in our hour of need. Fran Sandin has attended my classes through the years in Greenville. In her book, *See You Later Jeffrey*, she wrote of the funeral of her infant son:

> As the service ended, I realized God's finger was on my pulse. I was aware the Great Physician had placed me in His Intensive Care Unit. His celestial needle and thread were already mending my broken heart. His staff were caring family and friends on each side, holding me up as I began walking along the rugged road to recovery.
>
> At home, in the stillness of the night, my desire to hold Jeffrey was intense. Tears trickled onto my pillow as I softly cried, "Jeffrey is gone. What must I do now, Lord?"

> This Scripture came to mind: "I want you to trust me in your times of trouble, so I can rescue you, and you can give me glory" (Psalm 50:15 TLB) (Sandin 51).

David continued, "O my God, I cry out by day, but you do not answer, by night, and am not silent" (Psalm 22:2 NIV). Perhaps in part he was describing his own experience in the crucible of trial. But he surely captured the mind of Christ at Gethsemane and at the cross. No answer to the agony of the Son came from the Father. None could be given. For the final three hours of Jesus' suffering, the world stood in darkness. For three hours God blew out the sun and pulled the curtain because this was work for only the Father and the Son. One hundred and eighty minutes—it must have seemed like a lifetime. A twenty-six-mile marathon can be run in less time than that. Scripture drops a veil over the scene. We don't know the Father's thoughts, though certainly his heart was breaking. We hear only the Son's words. With a blackened sky to shroud him, the Son submitted and became sin for us (see Luke 22:41-44).

The Righteousness of the Cross

It was necessary that the Father withdraw himself from his much-loved Son. The reason was without doubt understood by Jesus, although a "Why?" escaped his lips. The answer was given by David:

> Yet you are enthroned as the Holy One;
> you are the praise of Israel.
> In you our fathers put their trust;
> they trusted and you delivered them.
> They cried to you and were saved;
> in you they trusted and were not disappointed
> (Psalm 22:3-5 NIV).

God is holy and perfect, "the praise of Israel." He is totally righteous, totally sinless, totally worthy of honor and praise. He cannot embrace sin. He cannot fellowship with sin; he cannot look on it. Thus he could not look on the Son when Jesus became sin for us. He had to withdraw. Nothing in the character of God is impure. Nothing is blemished, nothing less than spotless. And so he turned his back while his Son carried the sin of the world.

This side of Calvary, we cannot fully fathom the righteousness of God. We Christians are so entangled with the world, so enraptured by its allure, that we can't comprehend complete holiness. Our shallow worship and lukewarm complacency reveal hearts with misplaced priorities. We're often more interested in arranging compromises than in obeying commands (see 2 Timothy 2:3-4).

Even though that is so, we can still appreciate the power of a God who fulfills his promises. Look again at what David says about God in Psalm 22:4-5. He reminds us that his own ancestors trusted God and that God delivered them. It was God who convinced pharaoh to release the children of Israel from bondage in Egypt, God who parted the corridors of the Red Sea, God who supplied the water and meat and manna and clothing that did not wear out. The Israelites cried to God and were saved. They trusted in him and were not disappointed. Their experiences assure us that when we lay hold of God in prayer, we're connected with someone we can count on. "I am the Lord, the God of all mankind. Is anything too hard for me?" the Father asked of the prophet Jeremiah (Jeremiah 32:27 NIV; see also 33:3).

"My God, my God, why have you forsaken me?" came the plaintive cry from Calvary. David then added another detail proving that the psalm cannot consist merely of human reflections on human trouble. We're not just looking at a history of David's own hassles. "But I am a worm and not a man, scorned by men and despised by the people" (Psalm 22:6). How closely those statements describe Christ.

In previous chapters we've discussed how Jesus was rejected by his people, hated and scorned by the masses. The word translated "worm" refers to the coccus worm, a creature harvested and crushed for the red dye it produces. That dye colored the curtains of the Jewish tabernacle a deep scarlet. The creature is representative of Jesus. Viewed with contempt and disdain by the bulk of humanity, Jesus was crushed for us. Only through the shedding of the savior's blood was there any basis for the forgiveness of sins. In Hebrews we read, "Without shedding of blood there is no forgiveness" (9:22b NASB). So Jesus voluntarily left the palaces of heaven to die like a worm amid the dust and dirt of the earth, enabling us to read these words of Isaiah and claim them as our own: " 'Come now, let us reason together,' says the Lord. 'Though your sins are like scarlet, they shall be as white as snow' " (Isaiah 1:18 NIV).

> "My God, my God, why hast thou forsaken me?"
> Was the savior's cry.
> From heaven came the Father's voice,
> "No other choice have I."

II. Father, Forgive Them
Psalm 22:7-8

> All who see me mock me;
> they hurl insults, shaking their heads:
> "He trusts in the Lord;
> let the Lord rescue him.
> Let him deliver him,
> since he delights in him" (NIV).

The Contempt of the Cross

As David went on to chronicle the cross prophetically, he described the actions and attitudes of the onlookers to the

Lord's suffering. There were taunts, jeers, mockery. Let God save him if he can! Where's his God now? Ha!

Jesus knew it would be so, and that makes his willing sacrifice all the more marvelous, precious, and superhuman. Such scoffing continues today. Skeptics scorn him still.

Matthew 27:39-44 gives us the sad spectacle at the foot of the cross:

> And those who were passing by were hurling abuse at Him, wagging their heads, and saying, "You who destroy the temple and rebuild it in three days, save Yourself! If You are the Son of God, come down from the cross." In the same way the chief priests also, along with the scribes and elders, were mocking Him, and saying, "He saved others; He cannot save Himself. He is the King of Israel; let Him now come down from the cross, and we shall believe in Him. He trusts in God; let Him deliver Him now, If He takes pleasure in Him; for He said, 'I am the Son of God.' " And the robbers also who had been crucified with Him were casting the same insult at Him (NASB).

It all happened, just as David had said it would. "Come down!" they cried. "Prove yourself!" they taunted. He who could have summoned fire from heaven to consume them chose instead to remain aloft in agony. Instead, he uttered these words: "Father forgive them; for they do not know what they are doing" (Luke 23:34).

Let's briefly look at the events that have already transpired. Otherwise, we won't realize the full impact of Jesus' plea on our behalf.

1. Jesus shared the last supper with his disciples in the upper room; Judas left to betray him.
2. The Lord prayed in the garden of Gethsemane.

3. In the garden, Jesus was betrayed and arrested.
4. Jesus was dragged before Caiaphas and the Sanhedrin.
5. Peter denied him three times.
6. In the early morning, Christ appeared before Pilate for the first time.
7. Pilate sent Jesus to Herod (Luke 23:6-11).
8. The Lord was taken before Pilate a second time.
9. Pilate made an offer to the people to release either Jesus or an insurrectionist, Barabbas. The crowd chose Barabbas.
10. Jesus was scourged.
11. The Roman soldiers mocked him and thrust the crown of thorns down on his head.
12. The procession to Golgotha began.
13. Jesus stumbled under the weight of the cross and a man named Simon the Cyrene was made to carry it.
14. The Lord was nailed to the cross (9:00 a.m.).

When it came to insult and interrogation, the Roman soldiers knew how to do it. Their methods went beyond rubber hoses and blinding lights. They were pros. Their tortures were devilish, designed to pummel the body and destroy the spirit. It was with the last motive especially in mind that they fashioned thorny branches into a makeshift crown and shoved it down on Jesus' head so that blood streamed down his cheeks, mixed with the tears of a breaking heart. They continued the sick game of reviling his royalty by wrapping him in a purple vest, draping a scarlet robe around his bruised shoulders and bleeding back, thrusting a phony scepter into his hand. Kneeling in false obeisance, they cried, "Hail, King of the Jews!" Rather than gifts of gold, frankincense, and myrrh, they lavished him with blows. They spat at him. They jeered at him (Matthew 27:27ff). With that sordid send-off they led Jesus to the cross, the words from his sermon on the mount surely still ringing in his ears: "Blessed are you when men revile you, and persecute you, and say all kinds of evil against you falsely, on account of Me" (Matthew 5:11 NASB).

Out into the streets he staggered. The mob pushed and shoved him. Like the hunted caribou, Jesus, thanks to his all-night harassment by the pack of human wolves and his loss of blood, could run no more. He showed signs of yielding to the inevitable when he stumbled and fell beneath the load of the cross. The predators were winning. The smell of blood intensified the frenzy of the forces of hell. We've finally got him, they gleefully jeered. The battle was turning. God was losing, so it seemed. Like volcanoes waiting to explode, the religious leaders and caustic crowds spewed their bitterness and hatred at Jesus. How soon the hosannas turned to calls for his crucifixion.

The Compassion of the Cross

Then, at the hill called Golgotha just outside Jerusalem, the procession paused. The soldiers laid the cross on the ground and stretched Jesus across it. Each movement of his head embedded the thorns farther into his skull. His torn back scraped against the rough beams. Hammers were raised. Spikes split bone and tissue, muscle and nerve, as he was nailed to the cross. As the apparatus was jerked upward and dropped roughly into a hole in the ground, the Lord's entire body shuddered with wracking pain.

What did he say? "Father, forgive them; for they do not know what they are doing."

"Father, forgive them." Luke's version of Jesus' words indicates that the Lord spoke in the imperfect tense. The idea conveyed is one of an ongoing action. Translated precisely, his statement would read this way, "The Lord Jesus kept on praying, 'Father, forgive them for they are not knowing what they are doing.' " He kept on praying that God would forgive his killers. He prayed again and again for the ones who desired him dead.

I have trouble forgiving someone who cuts in front of me on the freeway, much less dealing with folks whose purpose in life is making others miserable so they can have some company. Letting go of resentments before they become causes for bitterness is critical, yet how long we sometimes hold on to things that should have been forgiven immediately. Jesus didn't have that problem.

It wasn't unusual for criminals to cry out from the cross. Often their statements contained pleas for mercy or protests of innocence. Not Jesus. He prayed for the souls of his accusers and abusers. Matthew 27 and Luke 23 give us the loathsome account.

Jewish religious leaders—high priests, Pharisees, scribes, Sadducees, maybe even Saul of Tarsus—looked on, hatred in their eyes. They mocked him. They insulted him. "Father, forgive them!" he cried.

III. Woman, Behold Your Son . . . Behold Your Mother
Psalm 22:9-11

> Yet you brought me out of the womb;
>   you made me trust in you
>   even at my mother's breast.
> From birth I was cast upon you;
>   from my mother's womb you have been my God.
> Do not be far from me,
>   for trouble is near
>   and there is no one to help (NIV).

Those Beneath the Cross

Think of Jesus on the cross, looking out over an ocean of angry faces, listening with broken heart to each insult. Was there anyone who cared? Could any identify with him? Was anyone left? Then his eyes fell on two who with a few other faithful had hung on for the duration, the only two of his most intimate circle to wait forlornly at the bottom of the cross and to share his suffering from afar: his friend John and his mother Mary.

How typical. When all is said and done, your disciples may desert you. Your friends may forsake you. Your nation may despise you. But your mother will be standing there. She won't give up on you. "Many waters cannot quench love; rivers cannot wash it away," wrote Solomon (Song of Songs 8:7 NIV). Such is the intensity of a mother's love for her own. The dedication of Patti Roberts's autobiographical *Ashes to Gold* is a testimonial to mother-love. As Patti's mother never turned her back during her daughter's traumatic divorce from televangelist Richard Roberts, neither did Jesus' mother desert him as the world mocked, misjudged, and murdered him. One object of mother-love is merely human, the other divine—yet the parallels are there. In her dedication Patti Roberts wrote:

> *To my mother, Martha Alice Holcombe Reames,* a woman who consistently lives her life with courage and dignity.
>
> It was she, pregnant with my brother, who kept faith after receiving a telegram from the U.S. Army stating that for the second time Daddy's plane had been shot down from the air over Austria by the Germans and he was missing. For ten-and-a-half months she held on to the hope that he was alive, and when the American prisoners of war in Germany were liberated by the Allies, there stood Daddy, thin and sick, but alive.
>
> It was she who held on, white-knuckled, as Daddy bumped his pickup truck over the rut-filled, muddy roads in the middle of the night on April 28, 1947,

> cradling me safely in her womb until they reached the small hospital in Durant, Oklahoma.
>
> . . . It was she who wouldn't hear of me running home to Mama during the troubled years of my marriage. And it was she who ran unashamedly to me during my divorce.
>
> It was she who went from being the proud mother of a well-known and successful gospel singer, wife of Richard Roberts and daughter-in-law of Oral Roberts, to being the mother of a woman riddled by controversy, incapacitated by loss, a fugitive of sorts in the religious world.
>
> I saw sorrow in her eyes, but I never saw shame (Roberts 1983).

There was sorrow in Mary's eyes on the day that Jesus died, but there was no shame. There was grief, but no thought of going away. There was distress, but never desertion.

And Jesus on the cross didn't forget his earthly mother. If David's words indeed reveal the Lord's thoughts at Calvary, then we know that Jesus remembered his dependence on the Father, and also reflected on his bonds with Mary. From the gospel of John we know that the Lord gazed down into the face of the woman who looked upward in wounded love. Mary stood powerless, helplessly wishing she could save her son, desperately desiring to extricate him from the pain. Horror-stricken at his suffering, her strength was sapped with each passing hour. Did she age before his eyes, as is the wont of parents who must watch their children hurt? Fran Sandin wrote of the agony of watching little Jeffrey suffer and die from meningitis:

> All I could think of was Jeffrey. I felt awkward as I stood at his bedside. I was a nurse, but this time the sick child was my son. I was his mother, and the oxygen tent isolated him from me. My greatest desire was to remove

> everything and everyone and just sit by the window in the warm sunlight, rocking him, comforting him against my breast. I wanted to kiss his forehead and say, "Mom's here, and everything is going to be fine."
>
> Instead, all the tubes and equipment necessary to his survival separated us, and I felt utterly helpless. He was pale and motionless. Over and over I thought to myself, That really isn't Jeffrey, is it? This is not really happening, is it? (Sandin 31).

Jesus looked at the woman who gave him physical birth, who was willing to be the vessel used by God in his plan for the redemption of humankind, the plan now culminating at the cross. Lovingly he said to her, "Woman, behold your son!" He wasn't asking her to look at himself. That would have been too cruel. Besides, she was already watching his agony as much as she was able. Jesus then turned to John, the disciple whom he dearly loved, and issued a simple instruction, "Behold your mother." We read in scripture that from then on, John "took her [Mary] into his own household" (John 19:27b NASB), willingly assuming responsibility to care for the mother of his dying friend. In this we see another example of the Lord's amazing love and wisdom. That he'd think of his mother in the time of his own great need was wondrous. That he'd ask John, the only one of his disciples to live to an old age, to care for her was remarkably wise.

Notice, Christ made mention of his mother at the end of his earthly life. The Old Testament predicted that the messiah would be born of a woman, but never did it state that a man would be his natural father. David could not have been talking about himself in Psalm 22:10 when he said, "From my mother's womb you have been my God." In only one case in human history has God entered the womb of a woman. In only one instance has God been the spiritual Father of someone before physical birth. Of himself David wrote, "Surely I was sinful at birth, sinful from the time my mother conceived me" (Psalm

51:5 NIV). The description applies to all of us. Only once has a virgin been the vessel of almighty God. Paul put it this way:

> But when the fulness of the time came, God sent forth His son, born of a woman, born under the Law, in order that He might redeem those who were under the Law, that we might receive adoption as sons (Galatians 4:4-5 NASB).

IV. I Am Thirsty
Psalm 22:12-18

Yes, God hung from a cross, but a man also hung there, a man who knew physical pain, a man who felt each stabbing blow, each throb, each wrenching agony. The single statement of physical need that Jesus made from the cross is this acknowledgment:

> After this, Jesus knowing that all things had now been accomplished, in order that the Scripture might be fulfilled, said, "I am thirsty" (John 19:28 NASB).

The Torment of the Cross

That was the only sign of frailty, the only statement of human physical limitation made by Christ at Calvary. He did it, as John said, "in order that the Scripture might be fulfilled." Yet we mustn't forget that he really *was* thirsty. He'd been on the cross for some six hours when he uttered the cry. Think of the loss of blood, the fever raging from his wounds, the weakness from lack of sleep and physical torment. The blazing Palestinian sun boiled away his body juices. No wonder he craved a cup of water. No wonder, as we read in both Psalm 69:21 and John 19:28-30, he welcomed a sponge soaked in sour wine to appease his burning mouth and parched throat.

How Christ suffered! No New Testament writer described

the horror of Calvary as graphically as David did in the verses that follow. How like God to do the unexpected! Eyewitnesses to the event do not paint so intense a picture of the agony as does a writer recording divine revelation one thousand years before the fact. Nothing in David's life paralleled the misery of Psalm 22:12-18. Let's examine the section verse by verse. So realistic are David's words that the text hardly needs explanation. The wonder is that Christ only made one cry of need. We are transported to the cross as we read.

The Onlookers

Verse 12: Many bulls surround me; strong bulls of Bashan encircle me. Have you ever been in a fenced pasture with an untamed bull? I'm no expert on the subject, but I was once in the same pasture with an immense Brahma bull. When he pawed the ground with his feet, I left. The adrenalin produced by his pawing allowed me to clear the fence with the ease of an Olympic high jumper, my Superman red cape flapping in the breeze! Imagine being completely surrounded by fierce bulls with no way of escape. That's how Christ felt on the cross.

The bulls of Bashan to which David referred were huge creatures, fat and strong from living off luxuriant pasture land. Many scholars believe that Bashan was where bullfighting first started. We're not talking about the type of bullfighting in Spain and Mexico. This is not the stuff of rings, matadors, mounted picadors, swords, fancy capes and fancier footwork. Bashan-brand bullfighting was man and beast alone in a large arena with a big tree growing in the middle. The fighter tantalized the bull with a scarlet cloth, getting the animal so riled up that he'd come snorting and charging. The fighter would maneuver himself so that he stood in front of the tree, and there would dangle the red cloth enticingly while the bull kept coming, enraged and out of control. Then at the last second, if there were no complications, the fighter would scoot behind the tree, and the bull would gore the tree, hopefully becoming stuck. When that happened, the bullfighter was the hero. When the bull only bashed his head and didn't become stuck, I imagine the bullfighter vaulted the fence in a way similar to my own exit. There's no sense hanging around trying to be a hero. Better to be a live chicken than a dead duck.

In Christ's case the great bulls of Bashan were those surrounding him with their jeers and taunts. He had already been gored to the tree, unable to sidestep the awful thrust of the horns if he were to fulfill the will of his Father. The bulls surrounded him, seething with rage.

Verse 13: Roaring lions tearing their prey open their mouths wide against me. Again David's figurative speech described the ravenous, onlooking crowd, hungry for warped justice, blinded by Satan, ready to consume Christ. There he hung, partially nude, stripped of any semblance of human dignity, the victim of their blood lust. The entire episode reminds us of Peter's description of Satan as "a roaring lion, seeking someone to devour" (1 Peter 5:8 NASB).

The Trauma, Fever, and Thirst

Verse 14: I am poured out like water, and all my bones are out of joint. My heart has turned to wax; it has melted away within me. Have you ever dislocated a limb? I remember one spring when my oldest boy Bobby fell while waterskiing and dislocated a shoulder. We were glad an orthopedic surgeon was driving the boat. A finger, a shoulder, an elbow—the pain is horrendous when even one pops out of joint. What if all your bones were dislocated? It happened to the savior! The rigors of the execution stretched his joints asunder, ripping cartilage and tendons. His hands, wrists, elbows, shoulders, pelvis, knees popping apart—the agony is incomprehensible.

Not only were his bones out of joint, but his heart "turned

to wax," melting within him. When the soldiers pierced Jesus' side, an issue of blood and water poured out (see John 19:34). Because of this, some physicians believe that Jesus may have died of a ruptured heart. This physical condition couldn't have been one befalling David; he died as an old man of seventy, and nowhere in scripture is he described as suffering from a weak heart.

Christ's strength ebbed away, "poured out like water." Dizziness, fever, festering wounds, lacerated limbs, gangrenous tissue, swollen organs, and bulging blood-filled arteries—the unnatural position made each movement wretchedly painful. And there is nothing to suggest that sleep could come. The Lord remained suspended between consciousness and the relief of unconsciousness.

Verse 15: My strength is dried up like a potsherd, and my tongue sticks to the roof of my mouth; you lay me in the dust of death. No wonder Jesus said he was thirsty. His strength was drained, his body dried up like a scrap of broken, useless earthen pottery. Perhaps the worst of it all was the thirst. His thickened tongue, swollen, dry, and splitting, cleaved to the roof of his parched mouth. Sweat pouring off him, his sun-baked body steadily dehydrated. He who could have commanded the heavens to shower him with cool rain chose to be obedient instead. Craving liquid, his raspy voice surely cracked as he said, "I am thirsty." In the single act of mercy shown him, a stick with rags soaked in vinegar was thrust upward and he tasted it to relieve the fire burning within (see John 19:29). Surely the "dust of death" seemed like a welcome retreat.

Wounds and Weakness

Verse 16: Dogs have surrounded me; a band of evil men has encircled me, they have pierced my hands and my feet. There you have it, one thousand years before the fact—the dreadful account of pierced hands and feet, the awful picture of beasts circling en masse for the kill. David's hands were never punctured, his feet never split open by nails. As we've read in Isaiah, truly "he was pierced for our transgressions . . . bruised for our iniquities" (53:5). In a future day another prophecy will also certainly come to pass, as Christ returns victorious: "And I will pour out on the house of David and the inhabitants of Jerusalem a spirit of grace and supplication. They will look on me, the one they have pierced, and mourn for him as one mourns for an only child, and grieve bitterly for him as one grieves for a firstborn son" (Zechariah 12:10 NIV).

Verse 17: I can count all my bones; people stare and gloat over me. The Lord on the cross had had nothing to eat since the upper room. His skin stretched tautly over his wasted frame. Semi-clothed, his bones protruded for all to see and gloat about.

The Gamblers

Verse 18: They divide my garments among them and cast lots for my clothing. The testimony of John, an eyewitness to the execution, records:

> The soldiers therefore, when they had crucified Jesus, took His outer garments and made four parts, a part to every soldier and also the tunic; now the tunic was seamless, woven in one piece. They said therefore to one another, "Let us not tear it, but cast lots for it, to decide whose it shall be"; that the Scripture might be fulfilled, "They divided My outer garments among them, and for My clothing they cast lots." Therefore the soldiers did these things (John 19:23-25a NASB).

Matthew, Mark, and Luke also include the incident in their gospels. It was the custom for Roman soldiers attending an execution to divide the belongings of the condemned among themselves. Four men were on duty; Jesus had five items of clothing, so they each took one garment and then cast lots for the remaining one. They threw dice to see who the winner would be, all while the Lord neared physical death. Talk about the hardness of the human heart. He was hanging in agony above them, and they were worried about who would get his coat.

Think of your own loved ones. When people draw near to physical death, we don't start trying to dispose of their belongings, do we? No. We want them to stay around as long as possible. Even the most money-grubbing heirs wait to make their moves till the dying one has become the dearly departed. We don't start giving away Grandpa's golf clubs or Aunt Minnie's china till Gramps and Aunt Minnie are no more. We wait a respectable time after the funeral to hold an estate sale or to divide the heirlooms among the heirs.

But the soldiers didn't wait for Jesus to die. Right beneath him, right beside his own mother, they grabbed the clothes he'd worn. Scripture had predicted it, but the coldheartedness still appalls us. Imagine watching others gamble for your property because you'd never need it again. The thugs got the spoils—but at what cost.

V. Father, Into Your Hands I Am Committing My Spirit Psalm 22:19-21

The Surrender at the Cross

As Jesus drew inexorably closer to physical death, he, "crying out with a loud voice, said, 'Father, into thy hands I commit My spirit' " (Luke 23:46 NASB). They are the last words Luke recorded of the Lord before death. The inspiration for these statements of surrender and submission must surely have been David's prayer in Psalm 22:19-21. There we read:

> But you, O Lord, be not far off;
> O my Strength, come quickly to help me.
> Deliver my life from the sword,
> my precious life from the power of the dogs.
> Rescue me from the mouth of the lions;
> save me from the horns of the wild oxen (NIV).

The statements are signs that Jesus was ready to let go. He signaled the Father from Calvary, and his spirit departed. The torment was ended; in death he found the release he longed for.

"Save me from the horns of the wild oxen" was the predicted cry. I wonder which oxen the Lord meant there. Was it the bulls of Bashan? Perhaps, but he was probably thinking of the horns mounted at the four corners of the altar of sacrifice in the Jewish tabernacle. In order to atone for the sins of the nation, the spotless lamb would be sacrificed according to the tenets of Jewish law. Its flesh was cut into pieces and hung on the horns of the altar in preparation for the burning of the sacrifice. At the cross, Jesus hung on the horns and asked for deliverance from the ordeal. He came to be our sin offering—yet how comforting it is to us, as we long for our own torment to end, to know that he desired his suffering to reach a conclusion also. He identifies with us totally. He knows us intimately. He understands.

VI. Today You Shall Be with Me in the Paradise
Psalm 22:22-30

The Hope of the Cross

The sixth of Jesus' statements foreshadowed by David in Psalm 22 was not the final sentence the savior uttered. But it was perhaps the most important, if such significance can be assigned. Luke 23:39-43 reveals that while Jesus was on the cross, two others were suspended on either side. They were common criminals, cheap crooks, guilty as charged. Like the venomous crowds below, they began to mock Christ, but then one turned to the other and said, "We are punished justly, for we are getting what our deeds deserve. But this man has done nothing wrong" (Luke 23:41 NIV). Touched by the Spirit of God, the thief next turned to the Lord and asked, "Jesus, remember me when You come in Your kingdom!" (Luke 23:42 NASB).

Remember me. Just remember me. That was all the robber asked. The Lord's reply? "Truly I say to you, today you shall be with Me in Paradise" (Luke 23:43 NASB). It wasn't too late for the thief on the cross. He was saved in the nick of time. His faith secured him an eternal resting place in glory with the Father. All he asked was to be remembered. God did the rest, exceedingly, abundantly, beyond anything the dying criminal could ask or think. Not only would the Lord remember the man, but the thief would dwell with him in paradise that very day. It is a promise of hope, an assurance of salvation. Like the thief, we believers will be with the Lord the instant we depart this life. We can count on his remembering us.

Does heaven seem real to you? Pearl and I were privileged one year to spend Christmas in the Dominican Republic as guests of the U.S. polo team. Our round-trip plane fare from DFW to Santo Domingo was paid for, and we rode modern shuttles to a luxurious resort hotel called Casa de Campo. Meals, soft drinks, accommodations, golf carts, green fees, caddies, side trips, sailing, boating, skeet shooting, tennis, horseback riding, and polo matches were all paid for by our hosts. What an unforgettable week. What an unforgettable forever it will be with our savior. He has paid the full freight for an eternal first-class experience.

Heaven is real. We can depend on God to do as he says. He'll remember the thief. He'll remember us. How do we know it's so? David put it this way:

I will declare your name to my brothers;
in the congregation I will praise you.
You who fear the Lord, praise him!
All you descendants of Jacob, honor him!
Revere him, all you descendants of Israel!
For he has not despised or disdained
the suffering of the afflicted one;
he has not hidden his face from him
but has listened to his cry for help (22:22-24 NIV).

How do we know that the thief ended up in paradise? It's because God responded to the Son. God "has listened to his cry for help" (Psalm 22:24). God raised Christ from the dead three days after he breathed his last. God took him home, stamping his seal of approval on the sacrifice of the Son. Jesus qualified fully as the redeemer, so we know that his words to the crook hanging beside him are true. We know that if we share the faith of the criminal, we too shall be saved. Because the Father receives the work of the Son, Jesus is free to provide salvation for a lost and dying world. Even the man unfit to dwell in civilized society, the man dying beside him at Calvary, became fit for heaven by the work of the Lord Jesus.

The Glory

Christ's shed blood is the accomplishment of his vows. The day of his glory is coming. David wrote of this in verses 25-30 of Psalm 22. It's glory we'll know if we, like the thief, become Christ's children in faith.

From you comes my praise in the great
assembly;
before those who fear you will I fulfill my vows.
The poor will eat and be satisfied;
they who seek the Lord will praise him—
may your hearts live forever!

All the ends of the earth
 will remember and turn to the Lord
and all the families of the nations
 will bow down before him,
for dominion belongs to the Lord
 and he rules over the nations.
All the rich of the earth will feast and worship;
 all who go down to the dust will kneel before him—
 those who cannot keep themselves alive.
Posterity will serve him;
 future generations will be told about the Lord.

In the future that we'll share with the Lord if we are his, the apostles will be there. The saints through the centuries will be there. There among the holiest of the dearly departed, amid the ministers, martyrs, and family of the faithful, we'll also find the crook from the cross.

VII. It Is Finished!
Psalm 22:31

The Completion of the Cross

Immediately after sour wine had been offered to Jesus and he had received it, he cried, "*Tetelestai*" or "It is finished!" and so succumbed to physical death (see John 19:30).

Tetelestai—it is the cry of a victor, a winner, a conqueror. It signifies the accomplishment of an arduous task. It describes the work of Christ, of whom future generations "will proclaim his righteousness to a people yet unborn—for he has done it" (Psalm 22:31 NIV).

It is finished, it is done, and if you're a Christian reading this, it's because Christ's righteousness has been proclaimed to you. It has been shouted from the upper rungs of Calvary. Jesus Christ can cry *Tetelestai* from the cross. The Father can cry *Tetelestai* when the Son is raised from the dead three days later. The Spirit can cry *Tetelestai* each time a lost soul comes to faith, each time a sinner stands redeemed in the presence of the Lord. When we take that step of faith, the Spirit marks *Tetelestai* on us for eternity. We're his forever, and someday we will see him as he is and we will be made totally like him. Thank God for finished work.

The Crosses of Our Own

Our psalm of the suffering savior began with a cry of agony and concluded with a shout of victory. Our salvation and redemption are a completed package. It lies beneath God's Christmas tree, waiting for us to reach out and take it. It doesn't come in pieces. It needs no batteries, glue, staples, or cement. It involves no complex directions. It requires merely that we accept it in gratitude. It's God telling us that the death of his Son was worthwhile so that we could have a relationship with him.

And what of that relationship? We're not promised a gravy train to glory, though some might preach that way.

Jeremiah wrote, "Is it nothing to you, all you who pass by? Look around and see. Is any suffering like my suffering that was inflicted on me, that the Lord brought on me in the day of his fierce anger?" (Lamentations 1:12 NIV). After reading about Calvary, we might ask the same question of Christ. Is any suffering like that which was inflicted on him? Is any sorrow like that poured out on our substitute in the day of the Lord's fierce anger?

Surely not.

At Round Top

Occasional shafts of sunlight pierced the cloudy gray January sky at Round Top Retreat in East Texas. The muggy weather made being outdoors uncomfortable for the moment, so the members of our Ministries board and staff, assembled for a mid-winter weekend of fellowship, filled an upstairs parlor of the conference center. Together that morning we prayed and praised and sang and shared joys and sorrows. I looked around the room, searching the faces of the dedicated men and women settled there. Two women, tragically widowed, sat next to each other. A retired couple whose children faced financial ruin lovingly and calmly held hands. Pain etched the face of a woman whose dear elderly father grew physically more infirm each day. Tears filled the eyes of her husband; his father-in-law had been the only dad he'd known. As prayer requests were related, incidents of divorce, child abuse, economic disaster, and grave illness were mentioned along with many praises to God. Ministry concerns were brought out. It was obvious that from this group of nearly thirty, volumes on suffering could be penned. What crosses they bore. What crosses we bear.

Yet no cross is so horrendous as the one borne by our Lord. Our human sufferings are insignificant when compared to what we've studied of Calvary.

We belong to Jesus twice. He made us. He bought us with his blood. Let's not forget it as we approach this season.

This Easter there will be some pain in your life. Much joy, perhaps, but certainly some sorrow. Your heart may ache over your children, parents, spouse, friends.

Remember, there is a sovereign God. There is a Lord who has been through the valley of the shadow and is waiting to guide you through it also. Remember, he bore a cross too. We can trust him. That's all he wants of us. Margaret Clarkson's poem "Sovereign Lord!" says it far better than I could:

O Father, You are sovereign
  In all the worlds You made;
Your mighty Word was spoken,
  And light and life obeyed.
Your voice commands the seasons
  And bounds the ocean's shore,

Sets stars within their courses
   And stills the tempests' roar.

O Father, You are sovereign
   In all affairs of man;
No powers of death or darkness
   Can thwart Your perfect plan.
All chance and change
      transcending,
   Supreme in time and space,
You hold your trusting children
   Secure in Your embrace.

O Father, You are sovereign,
   The Lord of human pain,
Transmuting earthly sorrows
   To gold of heavenly gain,
All evil overruling,
   As none but Conqueror could,
Your love pursues its purpose—
   Our souls' eternal good.

O Father, You are sovereign!
   We see You darkly now,
But soon before Your triumph
   Earth's every knee shall bow.
With this glad hope before us
   Our faith springs forth anew:
Our Sovereign Lord and Savior,
   We trust and worship You!

Reflections for the season

1. Are you, or is a loved one, enduring a time of trial and suffering right now? Are you bearing what seems to be an insurmountable cross? How does what Jesus did on the cross show that he understands what you're going through?

2. Describe the behavior of most of the Roman soldiers and spectators who witnessed Jesus' crucifixion (see Matthew 27:39-44). In what ways do people mock him still?

3. "It is finished!" the savior cried from the cross. Can he cry the same of you?

PART TWO

The Joyous Morning

C H A P T E R F I V E

The Record of the Resurrection

Mark 16:1-8

Seeing is believing, right? We trust the tangible. If we can't touch it, it must not be there. What we can't lay our own mitts on is considered fiction. We go along with pretending about the Easter bunny and Santa, for our kids' sakes, but we know they aren't really true. The danger is that sometimes, deep down inside, we think the same of the resurrection of Jesus Christ.

The Easter bunny, Santa Claus, the tooth fairy—in our society Jesus Christ is often relegated the same accord. We may stick plastic images of him on our dashboards; his silver form may grace our jewelry. His face sometimes beams out from heavy-metal rock albums stacked in record stores. We "believe" in him, *but* . . . surely much of what people say about him is myth. Yes, he was a man with intense spiritual insight, no doubt. Yes, he died on a cross.

But did he rise again? Impossible. It's a myth, a legend, a figment of the gospel writers' imaginations. Resurrection defies the laws of nature. It's absurd. Anybody who has faith in its reality is merely deluded. They're pipe dreaming. They're believing in the unseen, the extraordinary.

But that's what faith is, isn't it? Belief in the unseen. Belief in the power of a God to do the humanly impossible. Believing in the unseen—that's the essence of faith. Faith is the "assurance of things hoped for, the conviction of things not seen," said the writer of the book of Hebrews (Hebrews 11:1 NASB). But what about the *seen*? No twentieth-century Christian saw the crucifixion of Christ; none of us walked into his empty tomb, beheld his linen wrappings, touched his resurrected body—yet we believe. Is it some fairy tale in which we're placing our trust? The answer is no.

My point is this. When we place our trust in the truth of the resurrection, *we are not believing in the unseen.* You and I did not witness the risen Lord, but hundreds of eyewitnesses did. You and I did not journey to the empty grave, but many did. You and I did not place our fingers into the wounds on his hands and side, but others did. You and I did not drink and dine with him, but several did.

Is the resurrection real? Oh yes, it's well-documented. Scores of skeptics—General Lew Wallace, lawyer Frank Morison, and law student Josh McDowell included—have been converted to Christianity while trying to disprove the legitimacy of Christ's life, death, and resurrection. The fact is, if Jesus were tried on the charge of being resurrected from the dead, he'd be found guilty in any of our courts. The evidence of his resurrection is far more than circumstantial. His resurrection was essential. It was, as we've discussed in previous chapters, God's seal of approval on his sacrifice, God's saying, "Well done, my good and faithful servant," God's assurance that our debt has been stamped "Paid in Full."

Do you believe it? If not, keep an open mind as we look at Mark 16, John 20, and Luke 24. I'm betting you'll be convinced as we journey through these sections of scripture. And as we proceed, it should be with a prayer on our lips, "Lord, show us the glories of the risen savior."

Matthew gave the account, late in the Lord's ministry, shortly before he went to Calvary, of two blind men who said to him, "Lord, we want our eyes to be opened." Moved with compassion, he touched their eyes and they were able to see (Matthew 20:33-34). We must approach his throne with a similar trust and request. Instead of freedom from physical blindness, we must ask for our spiritual blindness to be healed. "Turn my eyes away from worthless things," the psalmist prayed (Psalm 119:37a NIV). Elijah said it too, speaking of a servant, "O Lord, I pray, open his eyes that he may see" (2 Kings 6:17 NASB). That should be the heart-cry of our souls. Jesus is alive, and because he lives, he is fully aware of what is going on in our lives. We're blinded by life, circumstances, our own natural abilities, our pride—and we overlook the Lord. We must come to Easter Sunday with hungry hearts, craving to know more about him, yearning for the resurrection to be real to us.

Another question we should ask ourselves is this, "Do I really know him?" Am I so excited about the resurrected Lord that, like Peter, I'd jump off a fishing boat and swim several hundred yards ashore just to look at him (see John 21)? Would I notice him in the mall, at the car dealership, in the grocery store, at the office, at my dinner table? Do I truly understand that the full force of the Father's wrath against my sin was poured out on him?

I am reminded of a story from pioneer days, when wagon trains traversed the prairies and the plains. As one of those trains made its way toward the new homesteads of the west, many in the group were startled by streaks of smoke crossing the horizon as far as eye could see. It quickly became obvious that a prairie fire was overtaking them and that soon they'd be trapped. Many of the settlers became hysterical. "What shall we do?" They had crossed a river the day before, but there would not be time to retreat to its safety before the fire would devour them. Only the trailmaster knew what to do. He gave orders that the grass in back of the train be set ablaze. As it burned, he ordered the wagons to move back on the place that had been burned by those flames. Onto the charred ground the wagons rolled while the prairie fire loomed ever closer. A little girl, still not sure she was safe, approached the wagon-master and asked, "Are you sure we are going to be all right and that the fire won't burn us?"

"Yes," replied the man. "You see, we are standing where the fire has already been."

What a picture of our peace with God!

> On Jesus almighty vengeance fell,
>   that would have sunk a world to hell.
> He bore it for a chosen race
>   and thus becomes our hiding place!

As Christians, thanks to Jesus' resurrection, we're standing where the fire has already been.

Looking Back

As Mark 16 opens, it's the Sunday following Christ's crucifixion. The Jewish day of twenty-four hours was reckoned from sunset to sunset; the Friday of the Lord's death was also the first day he lay in the grave; Saturday was the second, and Sunday the third. Let's back up a minute and review the events leading up to this hour.

A full week had passed since Jesus made his triumphal entry into the city of Jerusalem. The momentous occasions and traumatic circumstances, piled one on the other in seven days' time, undoubtedly lent an unreal quality to the entire week. Surely it all seemed like a dream, a terrible nightmare from which Jesus' followers longed to awaken. Yet it was all true. Only a week ago Jesus straddled the foal of a donkey and rode regally into his capital city. Only a week ago throngs of chanting people threw themselves down before him in worship. Only a week ago loud hosannas vibrated the city walls, a joyous crescendo of adulation soon grown still. Only a week ago the Lord had the world in the palm of his hand, or so it seemed. How could human nature be so fickle?

But it wasn't the Father's time for the overthrow of governments. He alone knows when the kingdom is coming. His greater purpose for the moment is the redemption of humankind.

After Sunday's procession the Lord entered and exited Jerusalem numerous times during the week, returning to Bethany to spend the evenings. On Monday he threw the money-changers out of the temple, cleansing his Father's house. On Tuesday he gave discourses in that temple, and also at the mount of Olives, where he predicted his final coming of judgment. On Wednesday the religious leaders conspired to frame him. Meanwhile, Judas made his ominous decision of deceit, and elected to betray him. On Friday (sunset Thursday), the Lord partook of a final supper with his closest friends, celebrating the Passover for the last time. Later in the evening he retreated to the garden of Gethsemane where he was apprehended. He was dragged before Caiaphas and, in the morning, before Pilate, who sent him to Herod. Then he was taken back to Pilate and Pilate offered to release him if the people so chose. Barabbas was let go at their insistence instead, and Christ was condemned.

By six o'clock Friday morning Jesus was scourged and spat on by the Roman soldiers. Judas, guilt-ridden, took his own life. Nine o'clock found the Lord hanging from the cross, his flesh split, his head wreathed in a crown of thorns, his life ebbing away. By noon the agony was unbearable. The world became dark and somehow, sometime, during the next three hours, Jesus Christ became sin for us. At three in the afternoon an unseen hand reached down to shred the temple veil, and with the cry "It is finished!" Jesus died. The earth quaked and rocks split. Graves yawned and expelled the dead, many of whom were seen walking the streets (Matthew 27:51-52). It was three p.m.; the sabbath began at six, and Joseph of Arimathea and Nicodemus barely had time to remove the Lord's body, wrap it in grave clothes and spices, and lay it in Joseph's family tomb before ceasing labor and observing the sabbath.

"Yet with a rich man in his death," the prophecy in Isaiah 53:9 about the messiah reads, and so it came about when Joseph of Arimathea, a member of the Sanhedrin or Jewish religious governing body and a secret disciple of Christ, gently placed the Lord's body in his family crypt. Joseph could no longer be a closet Christian. With his care of Christ's body, he made a public acknowledgment of his commitment. He considered the cost, and was there at the close anyway.

Who else was standing by while the Lord's body was lowered and wrapped in linen strips? Most left when the Lord surrendered his spirit to the Father and bowed his head in death. The stands emptied; the spectators filed out one by one. There was an eerie silence because everybody lost, or so it seemed, when he died. There was nothing left to be joyful or angry about, nothing even to arouse interest. The spectacle was finished. The clean-up was all that was left.

But a few onlookers remained. Among them were some special women. The ones mentioned by name in the gospel accounts are Mary the mother of Jesus, Mary the mother of James and Joses, Mary Magdalene, and Salome, although Mark 15:41 tells us that there were others, the faithful few who followed the savior to his final horror. These were the women who looked on in shock and dismay and disbelief, longing to relieve his torment. The men may, by and large, have deserted him, but these women watched the Lord die. They stuck it out till the bitter end. As Mark 16 opens, we're going to focus on three of them and how they responded to the Lord's death.

The Plan—Mark 16:1-2

> And when the Sabbath was over, Mary Magdalene, and Mary the mother of James, and Salome, bought spices, that they might come and anoint Him. And very early on the first day of the week, they came to the tomb when the sun had risen (16:1-2 NASB).

Bad news sets some women in motion. When the neighbor's husband suffers a heart attack, it's a woman who whips up cakes and slides pot roasts in the oven, offers to look after the kids, and volunteers for phone-calling, house-sitting, and chauffeuring. It's a woman who cleans the house, changes the linens on the beds, and takes home the laundry. At times of tragedy, most of us men stand around, thumbs hooked in pockets, eyes wide in wonder at the practical creatures we married. When it seems there's nothing anyone can do or say, women seem to know how to spring into action, and what sorts of action to spring into. The same was true in Jesus' day.

As the sun set on Good Friday, Joseph wrapped the Lord in linen sheets and conveyed him to his family's rock-hewn tomb, laying him inside and rolling an immense stone against the entrance. At sunset the sabbath began, and no work could be done then. So this was the most that could be accomplished with Christ's body. Other preparations were necessary for permanent burial, but there would be no opportunity till sunset Saturday. Oppressive silence enveloped the least joyous sabbath any of the Lord's followers had experienced.

But when the sabbath was over, at six p.m. Saturday, it was at last time to move. We read in Mark 16:1 that at the close of the sabbath, Mary Magdalene, Mary the mother of James, and Salome ventured out to purchase spices. The shops had opened. Nothing more could be done for the deceased Lord except to care for his practical needs. Today wives, sisters, daughters, and granddaughters select dresses, shirts, and suits to take to funeral homes for their loved ones to be buried in. It's the last tangible thing they can do for the deceased, a final act of love. Such were surely the sentiments of the two Marys and Salome. Their hearts throbbed and their eyes spilled over with tears as they visited the appropriate vendors. Their throats tightened as they tried to suppress their grief. They were glad to do the shopping for spices to be used in anointing Christ's body for burial. They wanted to be useful. Their consideration of Jesus' mother was evident also.

How painful it would have been for Mary, the mother of Jesus, to trudge along the city streets, peruse the shopkeepers' wares, and deal with the unpleasantries of actually readying her son's body for the grave. Some things are almost beyond the realm of the human soul to bear; the Lord's mother was surely spared more sorrow by her friends who were willing to help.

Who were these women? Often we conclude that anyone in scripture must be miles above us in character—spotless saints, pious Petes, and pristine Priscillas, never succumbing to human emotion, weakness, or temptation. We assume we can't relate to them. They're not like us. But as the Bible in candor and honesty reveals, that simply isn't so. These women were merely human. They would understand us, and we can understand them.

The first woman was Mary Magdalene. At least seven Marys are mentioned in the Bible—they're the Smiths and Joneses of the Old and New Testaments, and distinguishing them can be difficult. Mary Magdalene, as her name appears to suggest, probably came from the town of Magdala, just down the road from Capernaum at the northern shore of the sea of Galilee. Some have interpreted scripture to suggest that Mary Magdalene was a prostitute, an immoral woman, the "sinful woman" described in Luke 7:37-50. That cannot be substantiated, however, and it seems unfair to paint her as a prostitute without proof.

We do know from Luke 8:2 and Mark 16:9 that Mary Magdalene had been possessed by demons at one time. Satan controlled her. But she met Jesus Christ and he changed all that, casting out the seven demons that held her in bondage and healing her. She was a beautiful person with a terrible problem; the Lord dealt with that problem and Mary was never the same. She became a dedicated follower of Jesus, and it is a demonstration of the Lord's mercy and kindness that she would be the first person to view him in his resurrected body, as we'll later see.

The second woman was Mary, the mother of James and Joses. She was married to Alpheus, also known in Hebrew as Clopas. James was one of the apostles; often he is referred to as James the Less to distinguish him from James, the son of Zebedee, and from another James, the brother of Jesus who is credited with writing the New Testament book bearing his name. Confused? Just wait—here's more about Mary, the mother of James and Joses.

Remember that this Mary is described as the wife of Alpheus, a.k.a. Clopas? The apostle Matthew is called the "son of Alpheus" in Mark 2:14. Possibly this Mary was his mother also, although we are not certain of it. Many believe that this Mary was an older sister of the virgin Mary, Jesus' mother. If that is so, why would two girls named Mary be in the same family? Were the girls' parents just hung up on that name? Not exactly. More likely, if the two were sisters, the problem is with our translation. The virgin Mary and her sister Mary were likely both named after the Old Testament character Miriam, and their names were probably slightly different versions of Miriam—perhaps Mariam and Maria, or something like that.

If Mary, the mother of James and Joses, was not a sister of the virgin Mary, then it is likely that the third woman, Salome, was. John wrote in his gospel that beneath the "cross of Jesus stood His mother, and His mother's sister, Mary the wife of Clopas, and Mary Magdalene" (John 19:25 NASB). If the phrase "His mother's sister" is not a description of Mary, wife of Clopas, then it surely refers to Salome. We know that she went with the others to purchase spices for the Lord's body as soon as the sabbath ended and the stores opened. But regardless of whether or not she was Jesus' aunt, she loved the Lord and wanted to serve him.

Salome was married to Zebedee, and among their children were the apostles James and John, the "sons of thunder," as Jesus called them in Mark 3:17. These two, along with Peter, made up the Lord's executive committee. Salome is an interesting study herself. I think of her as the original Little League mom, so to speak, the first-ever stage mother. She approached Jesus and requested that he find a special place for her boys when he came into his kingdom (Matthew 20:20-23). She was thinking of an earthly kingdom, and desired James and John to be cabinet-level advisers—something like the vice-president and secretary of state, no less. She wanted Jesus to promise to let one sit at his right hand and the other at his left. If she was Jesus' aunt, why, he'd just be keeping things in the family. There's nothing wrong with a little nepotism, is there?

Salome had hopes, dreams, designs for her sons. The previous Sunday the Lord had entered the city a hero. The week had sped by in a blur, and now, unbelievably, he lay dead in a grave, the victim of his chosen people and a corrupt government. Don't you think she grieved when she saw him bow his head and surrender his spirit? Don't you think it stabbed her to the core to watch his lifeless body being lowered from the awful cross? Dashed dreams. Shattered hopes. A reality so far from her expectations that she could only be grossly disillusioned.

So what was she doing?

She was buying spices—keeping on keeping on, like the rest of them.

It's to Salome's credit and Mary Magdalene's credit and the other Mary's credit that they didn't lie in their beds soaking their pillows with bitter tears. Instead they did all they could do: they bought spices. And they arranged to meet at the Lord's tomb early the following morning, just when the sun had arisen.

What about you? Is reality so far from your expectations that you're soaking your pillow instead of searching for spices? What is your Calvary? A crumbling marriage? Mixed-up kids? Family illness? Shattered ambitions? Don't think the people in the Bible were always on top of the heap. Far from it. Many days they did well to inch out from under the rubble just a bit. Often the hurts were so deep that happiness seemed an illusion and victory an elusive ideal. Salome was there, for a while. So were the Marys. But they stayed in the game. They bought spices. The plan was all they had, for the moment. Soon would come a reality far exceeding their expectations. That's how things go with God.

The Problem—Mark 16:3

As the sharp first rays of the sun pierced the misty morning fog, the two Marys and Salome hurried toward the tomb of Joseph of Arimathea. On Friday evening, they pinpointed the location; perhaps they pictured the route in their minds as they tossed and turned, trying to catch a few hours' sleep. They approached the crypt as the sun rose, and before the grave was in clear view, paused to confront a problem. There was a detail they had overlooked, and they were worried. Recorded Mark, "And they were saying to one another, 'Who will roll away the stone for us from the entrance of the tomb?' " (Mark 16:3 NASB).

Surely the Roman soldiers guarding the grave weren't going to be any help. But you know what? The problem really wasn't a problem. Further, the women had wasted their money shopping for spices. There was no body to anoint, no stone to roll away. Yet Mary, Mary, and Salome speak to us in their quandary. They should make us ask of ourselves: How many of the problems we think we have aren't really problems at all, from God's perspective? How many of the things we're worried about aren't worth the worry, according to him? How many things is he already handling for us, in his way and in his time?

The answer is *all of them.* We've got to leave our problems in his hands. It means casting our cares on him, being anxious for nothing. Remember the words of the prophet Jeremiah? "Ah, Sovereign Lord, you have made the heavens and the earth by your great power and outstretched arm. Nothing is too hard for you" (Jeremiah 32:17 NIV).

When our teaching, camping, and counseling ministry was incorporated in 1972, Pearl and I had no money and three children ready for college. We also had no place to live and two children in junior high and high school. Talk about problems. We could do nothing but trust the Lord, clinging to his promise: "And my God shall supply all your needs according to His riches in glory in Christ Jesus" (Philippians 4:19 NASB). Guess what? He did. And he continues to be faithful to his promises. Great is the Lord, and greatly to be praised!

Problems aren't problems, with him.
Who will roll away the stone?
It's already been done.

The Power—Mark 16:4-5

> And looking up, they saw that the stone had been rolled away, although it was extremely large. And entering the tomb, they saw a young man sitting at the right, wearing a white robe, and they were amazed (16:4-5 NASB).

Mark went on to tell us that the women looked up and saw that a miracle had taken place. The guards were nowhere in sight. The stone had already been moved. The problem had been solved by a power greater than they could imagine. Looking up, by the way, is the solution to just about everything life brings to us. The apostle Peter could tell us a lot about that. When he planted his eyes on the Lord, he walked on top of the water. When he turned his gaze toward the crashing waves, he began to sink. "Lord, save me!" he cried, praying one of the shortest prayers on record (Matthew 14:30). He didn't have time for one more word. Jesus reached out and grasped his hand. A drowning man looked directly into the eyes of Christ and rose above the storm-tossed sea.

Looking up. Where we're looking determines the attitudes and feelings inside our hearts. When we really hurt, when the pain is intense, the suffering real, we look down, we look away. We don't want people to see us crying. Mary, Mary, and Salome knew those emotions well. They looked down as they approached the tomb, the direction of their gaze a reflection of their dejection and depression. Looking down, they neared the tomb.

And there they lifted their eyes to behold the impossible: an open grave, an unsealed tomb.

Into the crypt the women inched, eyes wide with wonder, lips probably gasping disbelief.

"Look, Mary!"

"What on earth has happened?"

"Who moved the stone?"

"Where are the soldiers?"

They were witnesses to the aftereffects of a miracle. Inside the sepulcher, their disillusionment dissolved into delight.

A young man clad in a white robe sat at the right. He was no ordinary messenger, but a heavenly one, an angel. The women were "amazed." No wonder. Their problems weren't problems at all, because of the power of God.

The Proclamation—Mark 16:6-7

The young man noticed Mary, Mary, and Salome, and spoke, saying:

> "Do not be amazed; you are looking for Jesus the Nazarene, who has been crucified. He has risen; He is not here; behold, here is the place where they laid Him. But go, tell His disciples and Peter, 'He is going before you into Galilee; there you will see Him, just as He said to you' " (Mark 16:6-7 NASB).

Notice the angel's words. He understood the women's amazement. We'd be amazed too. And then the angel told them three essential truths:

1. Jesus has risen.
2. Jesus is not here.
3. You can see where they laid him.

The Lord was gone, but his body hadn't been stolen or burned. He had risen. The spot where he had lain remained intact. The linen wrapped about him was still there; the piece covering his head remained also. He was alive! He had no need of shrouds or grave clothes. What a fact to absorb. What a truth for each of us to reckon with.

The verb tense is progressive. The angel was really saying something like, "But be going and be telling this news!" It's go and tell, not show and tell. They had no body to parade, only the miracle of an empty tomb to relate.

As we read the text, it's easy to overlook two brief phrases which are really jewels of God's grace, gems sparkling within a passage already glittering. Look again at what the angel commands:

"Tell His disciples and Peter." Peter was a disciple, but the angel singled him out. It's "and Peter." God wanted to make sure that Peter got this message. No doubt about it, he wanted Peter to know that he would find Jesus in Galilee. Why is that so significant? The last we saw of Peter, he had cursed and denied even knowing Jesus. He spat out vile profanity while not owning up even to being acquainted with the one he had followed for three years (see Matthew 26:69ff). As Jesus died on the cross, Peter was nowhere to be found. We don't read of his watching from a distance, much less standing next to John and the women at Calvary. On Easter morning, he must have been feeling lower than a snake's belly. Yet God understood.

Tell Peter. Tell Peter what? Tell him it was okay. Tell him he hadn't failed miserably. Tell him that God is a God of the second chance. He won't cut you from the team. He won't divorce you when you get wrinkles and cellulite. He won't demote you or deport you. Peter would get another chance. And another and another. All of heaven looks on and acknowledges the love of the Lord for the feeble and the frail and the flawed. It was okay for Peter, because his heart was right although his flesh was weak. It's okay for us.

You don't believe me? You're reading this and you figure God has given up on you? He quit trying to get your attention a long time ago? Too much water under the bridge? Too many broken eggshells, too much spilled milk?

Listen. God hasn't written you off. That doesn't happen till you physically die without accepting his salvation. Until then he's ready and waiting. His arms are open, outstretched, longing to embrace and welcome you.

"*Just as he said to you,*" the angel reminded the Marys and Salome. Jesus would go into Galilee just as he said he would. There's a principle here: things happen as God says they will. We can count on it. Abraham fathered a nation, just as God said he would. Ten plagues riddled Egypt, just as God said they would. The manna appeared in the wilderness, just as God said it would. A savior arose, just as God said he would. He is coming again, just as God said he will.

The Pull-Out—Mark 16:8

The angel had spoken. The women stood astonished. But sittin' ain't gonna get it done, as our camp cook used to say. So of necessity comes the pull-out. The women turned and ran outside. Wouldn't you? As Mark chronicled, "They went out and fled from the tomb, for trembling and astonishment had gripped them; and they said nothing to anyone, for they were afraid" (Mark 16:8 NASB).

The women were shaking like Ford fenders, an old-timer from our church at Emerald Bay, Texas, put it. Those who remember the Model T's know what he meant. They were terrified, speechless. Why?

I realized something for the first time when reading this passage the other day. The women were scared because they hadn't yet seen the risen savior. Eventually they would, Mary Magdalene a little sooner than the rest, as we'll see in the next chapter. And others would see him: all the disciples, a couple of Christians walking down a highway to Emmaus, five hundred gathered together in Galilee, his half-brother James. There were so many eyewitnesses that denying his resurrection is tougher than admitting its truth. They watched him. They touched him. They looked for deception, but there was none. They scrutinized his every move, but couldn't be anything but convinced.

He does what he says he will.

And he said he would rise again.

Critics may pick apart the gospels, poking and prodding for apparent inconsistencies. The more we learn of scripture, the more we see that any inconsistencies are not God's problems, but ours. They are products of faulty translations, or of our human inability to understand the whole of his word. And in the end it doesn't really matter, because all four gospels clearly present these two truths, essentials of our faith:

1. The stone was rolled away.
2. The tomb was empty.

Those facts alone ought to tell us that God was at work. Nothing can take that away. No critic can convincingly contradict it.

There wasn't much joy the night the messiah entered the grave. But after people began to see him again, and after they received the Holy Spirit within, there was a change. Incredible joy enveloped them. Just count the number of times the word *joy* appears in each of the gospels in the accounts of the resurrection and afterward, and in the book of Acts. There would be no ecstatic joy if there hadn't been a visible resurrection. There would be no changed lives among his followers. There would be no courageous Christians and willing martyrs, were there no risen Lord.

The resurrection is real. The evidence is indisputable.

The Four A's

For now, let me leave you with four thoughts about the resurrection and what it does for us.

1. The resurrection tells us that God is *alive.* He is *aware* of what is going on in our lives.

Your life is not some random happening. All things are open to the Lord. He knows every detail of our lives and he allows them to continue. He manufactures the air we breathe. He permits every movement in the script we unwittingly follow. He cares intensely about the decisions we make. Nothing affects or alters his love for us.

2. God is *active* in the universe around us.

He commands the angels. He is integrally involved in every facet of our lives, whether we know him as savior or not. The fact that you are reading these words right now is part of his plan. You think you chose this book? Maybe so, but he arranged it to be displayed in the corner of the bookstore where you looked. He prompted that friend to give it to you. He urges you to attend a church service. You may think you're going to impress your family or to appease your wife, but the truth is that he has worked the circumstances so you'll capitulate and come. After he gets you where he wants you, he'll always leave the final decision to you, but he'll get you to the place where you'll have a chance to decide. That you can count on.

3. God is *attentive* to our every need.

The Lord is the giver of the gift of life, and of everything else. He has created a universe uniquely suited to us, his creation. He master-planned a perfect environment for Adam and Eve, and he is in the process of preparing a marvelous place for all who know him.

4. We are *accountable* to him.

We can talk about accountability. It's a term we don't like much these days. But because God gives us chance after chance, because he arranges circumstance after circumstance to bring us to him, because all that can be known about him is evident in his created universe, no one has an excuse for ignoring him. Even an illiterate individual is without excuse. God will hold us accountable for our response to him. "It is appointed for men to die once, and after this comes judgment" (Hebrews 9:27 NASB).

Eat, Drink, and Get Ready

A year ago an issue of the *Ladies Home Journal* (not my normal reading) featured an article on one of my favorite entertainers. This well-known comedian has it all: a hit television show, a loving real-life family, millions of dollars in commercial endorsements. I'm referring to Bill Cosby. Let me quote from the article:

> But he [Cosby] doesn't despair at growing older. "It isn't sad, it's *funny*," he insists. "I think growing older is wonderful." Nevertheless, he now keeps a close watch on his health. When a recent physical showed that his cholesterol level was high, he cut back on butter and milk. "I rectified that because I don't want to die," he says. "Sure, I'm scared of dying."

> Cosby will probably need to live to a ripe old age just to accomplish all his goals. He's planning to write a third book, on love and marriage, and he'd like to make more films. He has said he will quit his series after two more seasons so that he can concentrate on other projects.
>
> No matter what he does, though, you can count on Bill Cosby to break still more records. Is he already thinking legacy? "I don't have time," he says. "I've lived a good life—and I don't think there's an afterlife" (Collins 141).

The article concludes with the observation that Cosby doesn't need an afterlife; he's found his heaven on earth. It left me cold, but this is what much of the world thinks. Let's eat, drink, be merry, love, work, and play, for tomorrow we die. This is all there is. It never occurs to some of us that we might just be wrong.

There *is* an afterlife—in the presence of God, or eternally suffering apart from him, tormented in a lake of fire. We don't like to talk about hell, but Jesus talked about it. He talked about hell as fervently as he talked about heaven. It's a place where there is "weeping and gnashing of teeth"—and that's the good stuff, you might say (Matthew 25:30 NASB). Hell is a horror of flame where a mere drop of cool water will be an unattainable treasure (see Luke 16:24). I don't know about you, but I have better plans for eternity.

God is a God of the living. Jesus Christ said it with these words, "I came that they might have life, and might have it abundantly" (John 10:10b NASB). He is also a God of judgment and justice. The apostle Paul confronted the philosophers on Mars Hill with a sobering message of their accountability before the Lord: "He has fixed a day in which He will judge the world in righteousness through a Man whom He has appointed, having furnished proof to all men by raising Him from the dead" (Acts 17:22-34 NASB).

The options for us? We can eat, drink, and be merry, for

tomorrow we die. Or we can eat, drink, and get ready, for tomorrow we may be ushered into his presence. Jim Elliot, a missionary martyred by the Auca Indians in 1956, put it like this: "When it comes time to die, make sure that all you have to do is die."

And if we are Christians, and ready to die, let's never forget that most of the people we meet each day are probably not. Most are lost. That clerk in the grocery store, that bus driver, the mailman, the neighbor across the street—most will never come to know Jesus Christ. They'll step across to the other side expecting the billowy clouds, pearly gates, and waiting angel wings they've been promised in the movies. It happened in *It's a Wonderful Life*, for goodness sakes. It may have been a wonderful life, but it won't be a wonderful death for them.

Getting Ready

Lamar and Barbara Muse have been special friends for the past several years. Lamar and I got acquainted through our Ministries' involvement at Emerald Bay Community Church. From my vantage point of the pulpit, I often watched him sitting in the pews. A crusty, self-made man, a tough-as-nails corporate executive, Lamar was hard to read. Had he surrendered to the savior or not?

Word came one day that Lamar had fallen from a pecan tree in his yard and sustained numerous injuries. At the hospital we had a chance to visit.

"Lamar, if you had died in the fall, would you have gone to heaven?" I asked him.

"If I hadn't, it sure would have been a bum deal," he replied.

We began talking about God's plan for a relationship through his Son. An hour later, Lamar invited Jesus Christ to come into his life. Now he knows where he'll be if the fall is fatal next time.

This Easter, and every day, Lamar is ready.

Are you?

And if you are, what about your wife? Your husband? That friend? Seize the opportunity of the Easter season to tell someone you know about the treasure you've found in Jesus Christ.

Reflections for the season

1. God is *alive* and *aware;* he is *active* in the universe around us; he is *attentive* to our needs. And we are *accountable* to him.

2. God is a God of the second chance. Remember, he even called again for Peter, who had denied him. What are some practical ways in which this truth can affect your life?

3. On the first Easter morning, the women worried about how to move a stone that had already been rolled away. This Easter, stop and consider the problems in your own life. Which ones aren't really problems at all? Which ones are you willing to turn over to God so you can wait and watch him work? In what ways is he teaching you to trust?

CHAPTER SIX

Responses to the Resurrection

John 20:1-31

For a preacher, Easter Sunday can be a bona-fide marathon. Mine is a marathon on wheels. The two churches where I regularly minister are located some twenty-five miles apart at Emerald Bay and Hide-A-Way Lake in East Texas. Easter morn means a sunrise service at Hide-A-Way at 6:30 a.m. A few handshakes later, it's time to hop into the car and speed—I mean, speed—along the country roads to Emerald Bay in time for the 8:15 crowd. (It's okay—I have a police escort.) The third service is back at Hide-A-Way at 10:30.

So Easters can be pretty hectic, even for someone whose occupation it is to proclaim the good news of Jesus Christ. I've got to be especially careful that the Lord doesn't get lost in the huffing and puffing. Each Easter service is an opportunity to reach many persons who normally do not attend churches or Bible studies (the "holly and lily" crowd, I've heard them called). They manage to make semiannual pilgrimages to houses of worship at Christmas and Easter. Most come out of some sort of sense of obligation: to appease their families, to ease their consciences, even to convince themselves that church is simply the same-old same old (a blowhard preacher singing the same song, umpteenth verse, a little bit louder and a whole lot worse!).

I hope and pray, every single Easter eve and morning, that God will use me to convey Christ to these folks. Their eternal destinies are hanging in the balance. Caring compassion is the need of the day. Their saved family members are praying for them too. But the simple truth is that I'll never communicate Jesus Christ to them if I can't convince them of the truth of the resurrection.

The Lord's birth was necessary, his perfect life essential, his death critical—and his resurrection the sign of God's confirmation that it was all enough. Without the resurrection we have a worthless savior, dead and buried. With it, we have a living Lord.

If you've ever studied any eastern religions, you know that the bones and relics of the founders are often revered. J. Sidlow Baxter relates the account of a rumor which spread throughout India that the bones of Buddha had been unearthed. When the supposed bones were brought to India's most sacred city, thousands of devotees thronged the streets to prostrate themselves before the skeletal remains. Noting that, a Christian missionary remarked to a friend, "If they could find one bone of Jesus Christ, Christianity would fall to pieces." How right he was. The resurrection is a cornerstone of our faith, the number-one piece of evidence that Jesus Christ was who he said he was, and that the Bible is what it purports to be: the revealed word of God. Without the resurrection, we have no legitimate religion.

Paul said as much in 1 Corinthians 15:17-19:

> And if Christ has not been raised, your faith is worthless; you are still in your sins. Then those also who have fallen asleep in Christ have perished. If we have hoped in Christ in this life only, we are of all men most to be pitied (NASB).

Still, we discount the resurrection, don't we? Do you want to know how the world views the raising of Christ? Several years ago *Time* magazine interviewed thirty people and asked them to rank one hundred famous events in order of importance. This is what they came up with. Number one was Columbus's discovery of America. Tied for fourteenth place were the discovery of the X ray, the first flight of the Wright brothers, and the crucifixion of Jesus Christ. Fourteenth place. We Christians should cringe at the thought that anyone could consider Kitty Hawk as significant as Calvary. But that's how humanity looks at the crucifixion, and also at the resurrection, which, incidentally, didn't even make the list.

The Resurrection Timetable

We can't afford to underplay the significance of Jesus' resurrection. The apostle John surely didn't. He wrote his gospel with the intention of presenting Christ as the Son of God, and chapter 20 is a personal, intimate account of the resurrection. It's a close-up news report, complete with commentary, on the most crucial event of all time, the event that affected the life of each character we're about to meet. We're going to look briefly at some of the hard evidence of Christ's rising, and also at the heart evidence of lives forever changed, thanks to the Lord.

We'll read about three appearances of the risen Lord to those he loved. We'll see him manifest himself to Mary Magdalene, and we'll view her response. We'll take a look at the responses of John, Peter, and the disciples, and finally, we'll watch as doubting Thomas is fully persuaded that Christ is again alive.

As we read in John 20, you may notice some apparent discrepancies between John's account and Mark's, which we looked at in the last chapter. Matthew's version of the resurrection is slightly different in places, as is Luke's. It's important to remember that there are no real inconsistencies. It's just that each gospel writer, under the inspiration of the Holy Spirit, focused on the details of the situation that most affected him. Each writer took a unique perspective of the events, depending on his purposes and where he fit into the scheme of things. Taken as a whole, the gospels fit together in harmony—and this we'll see as we read on.

Before we delve into John's gospel, however, it might be helpful to get the overall picture in our minds of what happened that morning. Doing so requires that we consider each of the gospel accounts of the resurrection, and understand how they harmonize. To interpret any section of scripture correctly, we've got to examine it in light of the rest of the word.

John opened his account of the resurrection by explaining that on the first day of the week, Sunday, Mary Magdalene came to Jesus' tomb early in the morning. Mark already told us that Mary was accompanied by at least two other women, another Mary and Salome. Luke added that a woman named Joanna was along as well (see Luke 24:10). But John mentioned only Mary Magdalene, probably because it was Mary who found and told Peter and him about the empty tomb, and who returned there with them.

Remember, Mark said that when the two Marys and Salome entered the sepulcher, they beheld an angel, who gave them a set of instructions. They were to go and tell the disciples *and Peter* that Jesus had risen. Quivering with fear, the women fled the scene, stopping to talk to no one. After considering each gospel, it is evident that Mary Magdalene broke off from the rest of the group. Perhaps she left the tomb a little sooner than the others. The women, without Mary Magdalene, left with joy and fear to find the disciples, and on the road Jesus appeared to them. When they touched him and worshiped him, Mary was apparently not with them (see Matthew 28:8-10).

Confused? Don't be. As I have said, just remember that

each gospel writer recorded what especially affected him or aligned with his purposes. Together, the accounts mesh and make sense. Before we proceed any further, let's use a little conjecture and come up with the probable sequence of events of the first Easter Sunday.

1. The resurrection occurred at or before early dawn on Easter Sunday. An earthquake shook the landscape, and an angel, face shining as lightning and clad in brilliant white, descended to roll away the stone from the tomb and sit on it. The guards quivered and became as "dead men," probably meaning that they fainted from terror (see Matthew 28:2-4).
2. At early dawn on the same morning, Mary Magdalene, Mary the mother of James and Joses, Salome, and Joanna carried spices to the tomb in order to prepare the Lord's body for permanent burial. They worried about who would remove the stone from the entrance for them, and on arrival were surprised to see that it had already been moved. Jesus had arisen, but the women did not know it. They entered the tomb amazed, and finding it empty, were perplexed (see Mark 16:1-4; Matthew 28:1; Luke 24:1-3; John 20:1-2).
3. An angel appeared to the women in the tomb, telling them that Jesus had risen, and instructing them to convey the news of his resurrection to the disciples. Luke tells us that two angels were actually there, bearing this message. Mary Magdalene apparently quickly left to find Peter and John. The other women soon fled in great joy and fear, rushing back toward the city of Jerusalem to tell the disciples. The Lord himself appeared to them as they ran along, saying, "All hail." The women touched him and worshiped him (see Matthew 28:5-10; Mark 16:5-8; Luke 24:4-11).
4. Evidently Mary Magdalene did not accompany the women as they returned to Jerusalem. She must have departed a little sooner—or perhaps she was a faster runner. Anyway,

she alone went to get Peter and John. She may have left the sepulcher before the angel's appearance, or, more likely, she heard the message but its full impact didn't register with her immediately. She seems to have heard the instruction, "Tell the disciples and Peter," since she ran to do that. But she didn't quite fathom that Jesus had arisen. She thought that his body had been stolen. Upon hearing her, Peter and John ran to investigate and she followed. The other women came along a while later and located the rest of the disciples. Listening to their fantastic words, the men at first discounted what the women were reporting (see Luke 24:9-11; John 20:2).

5. Entering the tomb, Peter and John found it empty. The orderly arrangement of the grave clothes convinced John that the body had not been removed by foes or friends, and he began to believe that the Lord was somehow alive. He and Peter then returned to the city. Mary Magdalene, who had followed them to the tomb, remained in front of it, weeping. Then she herself saw the risen Lord, who gave her some instructions (see John 20:11-18; Mark 16:9-11). This appearance of the resurrected Lord was his first, according to Mark, so it must be that the other women were still on their way back to the city when Peter, John, and Mary Magdalene came to the tomb. It was probably shortly afterward that he manifested himself to the women on the road to Jerusalem (see Mark 16:9-11; Luke 24:12; John 20:3-18).
6. Later that same day, Jesus appeared to Peter. He escorted two disciples to the town of Emmaus. He also paid a visit to ten of the disciples who had gathered together. Thomas was not present.

Still confused? You needn't be. It's important to remember that some of the events described above happened one on top of the other, within the space of minutes, even seconds, not hours. God must not care whether we pinpoint the exact chronology, or he'd have included a timetable in his word. We know what happened, and we can ask him exactly when and how it all took place when we join him in glory (assuming we still care about such details then). I imagine we'll be so busy praising him that thoughts of schedules and sequences will be far from our minds.

What are the essential facts of the resurrection?

> The stone was rolled away.
> The grave was empty.
> The angels proclaimed his arising.
> Eyewitnesses saw him alive.

For the next forty days, the risen Lord appeared to a multitude of witnesses. On Easter Sunday, he made himself known to Mary Magdalene, to the other women who followed him, to Peter, to two disciples on the road to the town of Emmaus, and to the apostles when Thomas was not present. Eight days later he joined his apostles when Thomas was there. Before he returned to his Father, he also appeared to seven of the apostles at a lakeshore, to eleven apostles and five hundred other believers on a mountain in Galilee, to James, and then to the rest of the apostles at Jerusalem. Then he ascended into heaven to assume his place beside the Father. After his ascension, he miraculously confronted Saul of Tarsus on the Damascus road.

But it all began on Easter Sunday.

John—John 20:1-10

> Now on the first day of the week Mary Magdalene came early to the tomb, while it was still dark, and saw the stone already taken away from the tomb. And so she ran and came to Simon Peter, and to the other disciple whom Jesus loved, and said to them, "They have taken away the Lord out of the tomb, and we do not know where

> they have laid Him." Peter therefore went forth, and the other disciple, and they were going to the tomb. And the two were running together; and the other disciple ran ahead faster than Peter, and came to the tomb first; and stooping and looking in, he saw the linen wrappings lying there; but he did not go in. Simon Peter therefore also came, following him, and entered the tomb; and he beheld the linen wrappings lying there, and the face-cloth, which had been on His head, not lying with the linen wrappings, but rolled up in a place by itself. So the other disciple who had first come to the tomb entered then also, and he saw and believed. For as yet they did not understand the Scripture, that He must rise again from the dead. So the disciples went away again to their own homes (NASB).

It was all too much to comprehend—the rolled-away stone, the empty crypt, the angelic messenger garbed in brilliant white. Mary Magdalene raced back toward Jerusalem, such thoughts as these probably whirling in her brain. " 'Go and tell the disciples and Peter,' the man had said, hadn't he? Go and tell. Tell what? The Lord's body is gone. Risen? No, someone must have stolen it. It's gone. What do I do? Peter. Go and tell Peter. Where is he? I'll look at John's house. He's got to be there. Peter—I've got to find Peter."

And so she ran along the rocky road. Her progress was swift and soon she was within the city gates. Breathing hard, she slowed up a bit and jogged along the streets till she reached the house where John lived. She knocked violently on the door, and when it was opened rushed breathlessly inside. There were John and Peter, and probably Mary, Jesus' mother, for whom John had agreed to provide. They had observed a gloomy Sabbath—*celebrated* could hardly be the right word. The Lord was dead, and their hopes, aspirations, ambitions, and ideals seemed to have died with him. They looked glumly at the woman who barged in panting, caught her breath, and then blurted out, "They have taken away the Lord out of the tomb, and we do not know where they have laid Him" (John 20:2 NASB).

Who were these men to whom Mary ran? Peter and John—with John's brother James—formed the Lord's inner circle. John referred to himself (John 20:1 and elsewhere) as the "disciple whom Jesus loved." It was John who hung in for the duration, who endured for the long haul. John was the only one of the twelve who stood with the women at the foot of the cross, watching the master die. It was John whom Jesus asked to watch after his mother Mary, a burden the apostle immediately accepted. It was John, the author of five books of the Bible, to whom the Lord revealed a remarkable scenario of events yet to come, and whose account of that special preview we call the book of the Revelation.

If John was the apostle Jesus loved, Peter must surely have been the one who made him laugh. Loud, brash, impetuous, sincere, stubborn, opinionated, appealing, Peter was the leader of the pack. He was always the first to jump into things, and too often found that the leaps carried him from the frying pan smack into the fire. When Mary found him at John's, surely the events of the past few days were playing and replaying in Peter's mind. He couldn't shake the memories; he would never forget his foul-ups. What was it Jesus had said in the upper room? Peter, by the time the cock crows, you'll have denied me three times. No way, Lord! He'd been so sure of himself. Then, after the arrest, in the courtyard of the Sanhedrin, that servant girl had accused him of following Jesus. I don't know him! he'd replied, not once, but three times. He'd even cursed. Then the cock crowed in the distance, and Peter's skin crawled. Sweat popped out all over. He felt weak, his knees buckled. He had denied Jesus, just as the Lord had said. He had failed. He'd dragged himself away from the Sanhedrin and Caiaphas, and run blindly through the streets. In the morning he heard of the condemnation. By three o'clock it was all over. The Lord's lifeless body slumped forward, and in grief Peter joined John for the most pitiful celebration of the sabbath ever. How could he have been such a coward? How could he have let the Lord down?

Mary Magdalene arrived, and we see a whole series of false assumptions. Peter and John were under the false impression that Jesus was still dead. Mary Magdalene was under the false impression that his body had been stolen. False suppositions are dangerous, at best.

How many times in your own life have you done what Mary, John, and Peter did, jumping to the wrong conclusion? A tough situation hits us from the blind side, and we say, "God, what are you doing?" We prematurely assume that he's punishing us because our dog dies, our son gets into drugs, our daughter turns up pregnant, our boss takes the credit for something we've done, our club nominates someone else for president, our engine blows a gasket. God must be getting even with us, we assume.

The fact is, however, God got even with us two thousand years ago on a cross on a little hill outside Jerusalem, there where the Son died for our sin.

When tough times hit, we've got to trust. We've got to realize that God isn't getting even with us, but only loving us all the more in the midst of the struggle. It should encourage us that even one who loved the Lord Jesus with all her heart, who walked with him, who sat at his feet and soaked in his teaching, even Mary Magdalene, jumped to the wrong conclusion. "They took His body," she exclaimed. "We don't know where it is." In her grief she misinterpreted the whole scene.

What happened next? John 20:3 tells us that Peter and John leapt to their feet and headed out for the tomb. They didn't calmly stroll there either. They slipped on their running shoes and took off. Verse 4 tells us that John was a little faster than Peter. Some commentators believe that Peter was older than John, but I figure he was just more out of shape. In my years as a runner and marathoner, I've encountered lots of older men who could leave me in their dust. It's my goal to be one of them, one of these days. Peter probably could have used a few hours in the gym. Evidently John was the one in training.

Besides, Peter had plenty of reason to be a little slow about finding the tomb. He was soaked in guilt-grease, coated with it. I imagine as the tomb came in sight, his running slowed considerably. The sight of the sepulcher pierced him to the quick.

Once at the tomb, John stooped to look in and spied the linen wrappings that had encased Jesus. Naturally reserved, John hesitated at the entryway, but not Peter. Overcoming his reticence, Peter reached the entrance and barged on in. He too gazed at the linen wrappings. But inside the tomb, he also noticed the face-cloth, which had been draped across the Lord's countenance, now rolled up and placed to the side (John 20:5-7).

Why did Peter and John stare at the grave clothes earlier worn by Jesus? Why did Peter gawk at the face-cloth? It's because no logical mind could fathom why a body would be stolen and its grave clothes left behind. No one stealing away the Lord's corpse would take the time to unwind the linen wrappings; no thief would remove the face-cloth and waste time rolling it up; no vandal would leave it lying neatly. Can't you just hear Peter?

"What in the world? This is strange. John, get in here! Quick! I've never see anything like it."

Whether Peter beckoned him or not, John overcame his shyness and walked inside the crypt. He too gazed at the rolled-up face-cloth, and then, as he told us, he "saw and believed" (John 20:8 NASB).

What did John believe? It must be that at least the seeds of faith in the resurrection had been planted and began to germinate. Things the Lord said perhaps began rushing back to John. Perhaps Psalm 16:10 came to his mind: "Because you will not abandon me to the grave, nor will you let your Holy One see decay" (NIV).

It was all beginning to make sense, at least to John. Oh, he didn't have the whole picture, for John 20:9 states that "as yet they did not understand the Scripture, that He must rise again from the dead" (NASB). Notice, John didn't say, "We did not understand," but, "They did not understand," possibly referring to Peter and the rest of the Lord's disciples and followers. John knew that something wonderful, marvelous, miraculous, had happened. He was convinced that the tomb was empty, and that the Lord's body had not been stolen away. He probably realized that some sort of resurrection could have occurred, but he certainly didn't have all the pieces of the puzzle. Soon, very soon, it would all make sense. John 20:10 tells us that Peter and John returned to their own homes. Perhaps they discussed the incredible scene on their way back; maybe they mused silently on the weird chain of events that alternately devastated them and then dangled hope before them. Surely they shook their heads in wonder.

Where did they go? Back home, yes. And I'm convinced that the first person they probably sought out was Mary, Jesus' mother. They must have wanted to comfort her. By now she'd probably heard rumors and reports of the empty tomb. They wanted to reassure her that the body was indeed gone, that the evidence suggested that something as fantastic as a resurrection might have taken place.

John believed. Those simple words may indicate that he was the first Christian, as we use the term, in scripture. At least he was the first to believe in the reality of the Lord's resurrection. How calmly he arrived at his conclusions. If this was his conversion, how gently it came about. No fireworks, no lightning bolts from heaven, no goose bumps, no emotionally charged rollercoaster experiences. John just assimilated the evidence. And then he believed, without crisis, tears or tantrums, folderol or fancy. God sometimes has to use the dramatic to draw us to him, but how he must also be pleased by the quiet trust of a conversion like John's.

Mary Magdalene—John 20:11-18

> But Mary was standing outside the tomb weeping; and so, as she wept, she stooped and looked into the tomb; and she beheld two angels in white sitting, one at the head, and one at the feet, where the body of Jesus had been lying. And they said to her, "Woman, why are you weeping?" She said to them, "Because they have taken away my Lord, and I do not know where they have laid Him." When she had said this, she turned around, and beheld Jesus standing there, and did not know that it was Jesus. Jesus said to her, "Woman, why are you weeping? Whom are you seeking?" Supposing Him to be the gardener, she said to Him, "Sir, if you have carried Him away, tell me where you have laid Him, and I will take Him away." Jesus said to her, "Mary!" She turned and said to Him in Hebrew, "Rabboni!" (which means, Teacher). Jesus said to her, "Stop clinging to Me; for I have not yet ascended to the Father; but go to my brethren and say to them, 'I ascend to My Father and your Father, and My God and your God.' " Mary Magdalene came, announcing to the disciples, "I have seen the Lord," and that He had said these things to her (NASB).

Winded from her run into the city, Mary Magdalene could not keep up with Peter and John as they sped to the tomb. Sometime after they entered and observed the grave clothes, she arrived. Peter and John, lost in wonder and awe, evidently said nothing to Mary as they exited the tomb and headed back to town. Mary stood forlornly outside the crypt, eyes fiery red, tears streaming down her face. She stationed herself there at the entrance of the tomb, not wanting to give up hope that someone could provide a clue as to the whereabouts of the Lord's body. Peter and John weren't talking. Perhaps somebody with information might come along.

Stooping down, Mary peered inside, to behold a marvelous sight. Two angels, clad in white, now sat where the Lord's body had lain—one at the head, the other at the foot. They did not appear to Peter and John. But even this vision didn't quench Mary's tears. "Woman, why are you weeping?" the angels asked (John 20:13 NASB).

The angels had a right to ask that question. They knew of the resurrection. They were there to announce it. How dismayed they must have been to see someone crying instead of believing that the Christ had done what he said he would do.

"Because they have taken away my Lord, and I do not know where they have laid Him," she replied (John 20:13). Arthur Brisbane depicts a crowd of grieving caterpillars. Clad in black, the caterpillars wail in grief over the empty cocoon of a dearly departed caterpillar, never realizing that above the whole gloomy procession a brightly hued butterfly soars into the heavens. Our own funerals can be like that. How easy it is for us to focus on the cocoon, the shell that encased a Christian brother or sister, and forget that he or she is soaring in the heavens, truly free for the first time.

Mary grieved, like countless others who are sobbing over things they should not be sobbing over. She was fearful about something she need not fear. She was a victim of a false assumption. In her mind, there was only one explanation for the empty tomb: the men who nailed him to the cross had spirited away his body. There was no room in the inn when he was born; he had possessed no earthly home; now he wasn't even allowed a decent burial.

Having said these things, John's gospel tells us that Mary turned around and observed Jesus standing behind her, although she didn't immediately recognize him (John 20:14). Why didn't Mary recognize Jesus at first? Her grief wouldn't let her. Her vision was blurred by tears; her mind was blinded by presuppositions. Who could believe in the possibility of a resurrection? A living, breathing Lord was the last person she expected to see. In fact, when Jesus spoke, saying, "Woman, why are you weeping? Whom are you seeking?" she assumed that he was the gardener (John 20:15 NASB).

Someone had removed the body. Yes, it must have been the gardener. Such a removal would make sense. He was out watering the flowers and pulling weeds, readying the cemetery for Sunday visitors, and he must have placed the body elsewhere so he could sweep out the tomb.

How easy it is for us to ignore the evidence of the supernatural when a natural hypothesis crops up. We let the natural get to us. We accept natural outcomes as inevitable. We forget to look for a God "out there" who is interested in our daily lives and who is capable of serving up supernatural solutions to our problems. No job? The economy is flat? Can't get even an interview? How easy to assume that our family will starve. And then, miraculously, a temporary job or two comes. Money from Christian friends is anonymously placed in our mailbox. Our house suddenly sells in a dead-as-a-doornail market. Debtors begin to repay what they owe, with no provocation to do so. Opportunities emerge that were unimaginable only months before. You say it can't happen? But it does, time and time again.

The supernatural? The Lord was looking Mary Magdalene in the face, but she still assumed the unlikely.

"Sir, if you have carried Him away," Mary said to the Lord, still thinking he was the gardener, "tell me where you have laid Him, and I will take Him away" (20:15 NASB).

As we approach John 20:16, we are treading on emotional ground, on private, tender territory. The Lord allows us to peer behind the veil at one of the most beautiful, heartwarming scenes of his love ever recorded. "Mary!" Jesus said, his words piercing the fog of her confusion as she finally saw him for who he was. His use of her name confirmed the fact that the man before her was not just a gardener. Her bitter tears abated.

"Rabboni!" she exclaimed to him in Hebrew, a term meaning "teacher, master, lord" (John 20:16). The emotion of that moment overwhelmed her. Clinging to him, her tears of grief replaced by sweet streams of joy, she heard his voice as if for the first time. She knew now that he was alive.

Reading this account thrills me with anticipation of heaven. Once we believers are there, we'll hear and recognize many voices we haven't heard in a long time. My dad will speak to me. I'll hear the precious voice of my dear grandmother who first told me about Jesus. Somehow we'll know them, as we gather around the throne to worship the lamb.

Her arms around Jesus, Mary's emotions overflowed. From crucifixion to resurrection—it was all too much to comprehend. Patiently the Lord guided her out of her grief into the glory of what he wanted to reveal. He is a living Christ, the Son of God. Finally she realized that his sovereign hand was behind it all.

"Stop clinging to Me," Jesus gently instructed her, "for I have not yet ascended to the Father; but go to My brethren, and say to them, 'I ascend to My Father and your Father, and My God and your God' " (20:17 NASB). And Mary did that immediately, quickly. Refreshed and invigorated by her encounter with the savior, I imagine she ran faster into Jerusalem than ever before, even faster than earlier in the morning after she and the other women discovered the empty tomb. She took off to find the disciples and give them the story which the other women would reinforce after the Lord appeared to them also.

The Disciples—John 20:19-23

> When therefore it was evening, on that day, the first day of the week, and when the doors were shut where the disciples were, for fear of the Jews, Jesus came and stood in their midst, and said to them, "Peace be with you." And when He had said this, He showed them both His hands and His side. The disciples therefore rejoiced when

> they saw the Lord. Jesus therefore said to them again, "Peace be with you; as the Father has sent Me, I also send you." And when He had said this, He breathed on them, and said to them, "Receive the Holy Spirit. If you forgive the sins of any, their sins have been forgiven them; if you retain the sins of any, they have been retained" (NASB).

Can't you just see Mary flying into town, scurrying through the streets to find the disciples? She was so excited, she could hardly stand it. She had received living water, and she wanted everyone to know about it. Remember that the other women who had gone to the tomb in the morning also returned to town to locate the disciples. Sometime during their trip back, the Lord had appeared to them as well, and they too were ecstatic with joy.

Men, take just a minute and imagine your wife when she is excited about something that's happened at school, church, the mall, or on the job. She blows into the house bubbling over about a big sale, a possible promotion, a new program at church, an insight she's had during Bible study. What do you usually do? Jump up and down with her? No. Do you even pretend to be enthusiastic? Uh uh. Either you say, "That's nice," and go about your business, or you tell her, "Calm down, honey. Now, what happened? Give it to me straight. Without emotion, please." And you listen with that ear of unbelief, unimpressed, in the process throwing buckets of water on her enthusiasm. That's the kind of reception the disciples gave Mary Magdalene and the other women when they burst into the gathering place with their wondrous news.

Talk about raining on someone's parade. The disciples were experts at dampening the mood. Luke 24:11 says that the women's "words appeared to them [the disciples] as nonsense, and they would not believe them" (NASB). Given the same set of circumstances, we would probably react as the disciples did.

Our human minds reject anything we don't understand and can't explain.

With that sort of response from the men he'd spent the most time with, the Lord knew he had to do something to deal with their unbelief. First Corinthians 15:5 tells us that sometime later that day, he appeared to Peter, and we know from Luke 24 that he also manifested himself to two others heading for Emmaus. And that evening he acted to erase the doubts of most of the rest of his inner circle.

Picture the scene. Probably by Easter evening that time the disciples had just about convinced the women that they were dreaming. All but Mary Magdalene—I have a feeling she never swayed in her convictions. Most of the disciples were gathered together, perhaps having celebrated the sabbath with one another. Perhaps Peter had burst in to tell them he'd seen the risen Lord, but they recovered themselves and probably began to doubt again. Peter could be such a hothead, after all. Guilt plays tricks on you. Only ten of the original twelve were there: Judas had already committed suicide, and Thomas was off somewhere. So Peter, Andrew, James, John, Philip, Bartholomew (a.k.a. Nathanael), Simon the zealot, Judas Thaddeus Lebbeus, Matthew, and James the Less were sitting together in a quiet house. The shades and doors were shut because these brave followers of Jesus were afraid of the Jews. You can't really blame them for being scared; surely animosity was running high against anyone who had followed that "insurrectionist/heretic" Jesus who had been crucified.

How gracious of the Lord that he condescended to the disciples' disbelief. Into their midst he suddenly appeared, revealing himself to them in his resurrected body, greeting them with "Peace be to you" (John 20:21). Having said that, the Lord showed them his wounded hands and his side. Yes, it was Jesus! The disciples rejoiced at the sight.

Of course they were happy. Ten men who had seen their whole purpose in life shattered on a little hill outside Jerusalem—ten men who'd lost their direction. Now suddenly, miraculously, their leader was back. Imagine their joyous comments:

"Lord, you're back!"

"Where have you been?"

"The last we heard you'd been placed in Joseph's tomb. You died on the cross!"

"What happened? Tell us about it, please!"

Surely everyone talked a mile a minute, throwing questions his way—it must have been worse than a presidential press conference. Everyone wanted to say something. And so the Lord had to interrupt them and say, in verse 21, "Peace be with you; as the Father has sent Me, I also send you" (NASB). A better translation of the last half of that verse is: "I also am sending you." The action is progressive, ongoing. What did the Lord mean?

For one thing, Jesus was telling them that he wasn't through with them yet. They hadn't lost their jobs just because they'd deserted him when the going got tough. They weren't fired for sleeping in the garden of Gethsemane; they weren't issued pink slips for failing to testify in his behalf or for steering clear of the cross. His attitude toward them had not changed, in spite of their failings. They would always fail, in fact, but God would also always love them.

Indeed, Jesus had a mission for those men. Eventually, those ten, plus Thomas and Paul, would be known as the apostles. Their qualifications? They'd seen the risen Christ and had been personally acquainted with his earthly ministry (see Acts 1:21-22).

They were the sent ones. As Jesus began to explain in his first postresurrection appearance to the group, he was sending them.

Where? As we'll see later, to the ends of the world.

Why? To tell others about him. They would be witnesses.

What would it involve? As Jesus was sent to die, so each of the twelve would die a martyr's death, except John.

As Jesus was telling them, they were going to be different

now that he had died and arisen. They would be better. Once deserters in the midst of crisis, they would not forsake him again.

A Gift of the Spirit

Having said this to his men, scripture reveals that the Lord "breathed on them, and said to them, 'Receive the Holy Spirit' " (20:22 NASB). That phrase has been often misunderstood. In Old Testament times God allowed his Spirit to come on certain individuals, like Samson, Saul, and David, to empower them to perform acts of service. With God's Spirit, Samson killed a thousand enemy Philistines with the jawbone of an ass; Saul and David were anointed to reign as king (see Judges 13:24-25; 15:14-16; 16:20; 1 Samuel 10:6-7; 16:13; Psalm 51:11). After a task was completed, the Spirit would depart from those he had assisted.

The God of the Old Testament is also the God of the New, but he now gives every Christian his Spirit as an indwelling power source. The promise of the Spirit was made by Jesus in John 14:16-17:

> And I will ask the Father, and He will give you another Helper, that He may be with you forever; that is the Spirit of truth, whom the world cannot receive, because it does not behold Him or know Him, but you will know Him because He abides in you, and will be in you (NASB).

The Spirit is the regenerator and lifegiver who comes miraculously to reside within us at the moment we come to faith in Christ. Before then he acted to convict us of our sin (John 16:7-13).

After we enter the family of faith, he becomes our guide and comforter. He enables us to act as we ought to act, to think as we ought to think. He illumines scripture, revealing its meaning to us as we read. He brings verses we have memorized to mind as we need them. "But the Helper, the Holy Spirit, whom the Father will send in My name, He will teach you all things, and bring to your remembrance all that I said to you," Jesus said to his disciples (John 14:26 NASB).

The Spirit is an intercessor too, translating our prayers into correct requests for presentation to the Father (Romans 8:26-27). The Holy Spirit is one-third of the trinity, the three-in-one God we worship. He is coequal with the Son and the Father, but his function is different. Thank God, he is our resident teacher, illuminating scripture so we can understand and grow into Christ-likeness.

When Jesus predicted the coming of the Holy Spirit to indwell his followers, he did so during his last conversation with them in the upper room, just hours before his arrest and execution (John 14:16-17). When the Lord first appeared to the assembled disciples in his resurrected state, he breathed on them and they received the Holy Spirit to sustain them. It was a prelude to the permanent indwelling of all Christians that would take place on the day of Pentecost, after Jesus ascended into heaven (see Acts 2).

The disciples' joyous response to the sight of their king resulted in a commission for service. They were to spread the news of his salvation. Jesus summed up the main goal as he continued to speak: "If you forgive the sins of any, their sins have been forgiven them; if you retain the sins of any, they have been retained" (John 20:23 NASB).

Some are shocked by that statement. Were the disciples given that much authority—even to forgive sins? But that's not what the verse, or the Lord, means. A precise translation of the text reads, "If the sins of any you forgive, they have been previously forgiven them; if the sins of any you retain, they have been previously retained." The Lord's point was that as the disciples went forth to proclaim the gospel, some listeners would repent and ask Christ to be their savior. Their sins would be forgiven. Others who heard the gospel message would do nothing with it. They would not come to Christ in faith. Their sins would be retained. God is the one who is offended by our sin, rebellion, and indifference. God is the one who has the prerogative to forgive or not to forgive. His ministers can only announce it. His followers can only explain his plan for forgiveness; they cannot forgive or choose not to forgive. Each of us must come to Calvary just as we are, sinners condemned to die. At the cross we find that Christ has secured our pardon and extends his hand, holding the gift. It is ours for the taking.

Taking that message to the people—that is what Jesus empowers those who love him to do. That is what he enabled the disciples to do, so long ago. That is why he gave them the Holy Spirit. What a transformation! What started as ten depressed, aimless men hiding in a closed house, shaking in fear of reprisal from the Jews, became, after beholding the risen Christ, followers on fire for their Lord.

We've said that most suffered martyrs' deaths. Would they have been so willing to die for him had they not seen him face to face? Before his resurrection, most were too scared to stand within a mile of the cross. No lie, no myth, no figment of their imaginations, could have wrought such incredible change. Myths, conjectures, traditions, and suppositions are not enough to motivate a martyr. Christ is. As Dietrich Bonhoeffer, a German theologian murdered in a concentration camp by the Nazis, wrote six years before his death, "When Christ calls a man, he bids him come and die."

Thomas—John 20:24-31

> But Thomas, one of the twelve, called Didymus, was not with them when Jesus came. The other disciples therefore were saying to him, "We have seen the Lord!" But he said to them, "Unless I shall see in His hands the imprint of the nails, and put my finger into the place of the nails, and put my hand into His side, I will not believe." And after eight days again His disciples were

> inside, and Thomas with them. Jesus came, the doors having been shut, and stood in their midst, and said, "Peace be with you." Then He said to Thomas, "Reach here your finger, and see My hands; and reach here your hand, and put it into My side; and be not unbelieving, but believing." Thomas answered and said to Him, "My Lord and my God!" Jesus said to him, "Because you have seen Me, have you believed? Blessed are they who did not see, and yet believed" (NASB).

As was noted before, two of the original twelve disciples missed out on the incredible appearance of the Lord. Judas Iscariot had hanged himself, not realizing that the Lord could forgive him too. Thomas was also absent. Before we read what John had to say, we've got to understand a little bit about Thomas. He's one of my favorite characters in the New Testament, a loyal melancholic if ever there was one.

In John 11 we read the account of how the Lord had nearly been stoned to death and the whole crew had barely escaped with their lives to Galilee, when word from Martha and Mary came with news that Lazarus was dead. When Jesus announced his intention to go back to Judea, there were rumblings among the disciples. "Lord, you can't go back there! You mean you'll let them kill you?" But Thomas didn't grumble or rebel. He was as loyal as they come, although his commitment was steeped in pessimism. What did he say? "Let us also go, that we may die with Him" (John 11:16 NASB). In other words, "Okay, guys, let's follow him to the grave!" Not much comfort in those words, is there? But there is great commitment.

Thomas was the one in the upper room who had to know *why.* Jesus said, "I go to prepare a place for you. And if I go and prepare a place for you, I will come again, and receive you to Myself; that where I am, there you may be also. And you know the way where I am going" (John 14:2-4 NASB). To that, Thomas said, "Lord," stopping Jesus in mid-thought, practically interrupting him. "Lord, we do not know where You are going; how do we know the way?" (John 14:5 NASB). That's typical Thomas. He had to have all the details. I'm so glad he asked that question, because Jesus' reply is one of the greatest in the whole Bible: "I am the way, and the truth, and the life; no one comes to the Father but through Me" (John 14:6 NASB).

Thomas's commitment to the Lord was genuine. He'd made the commitment to follow Jesus, to death if necessary, back when the Lord prepared to return to Mary and Martha. He walked with the rest of the disciples and Jesus to the garden of Gethsemane on the night the Lord was arrested. I think that Thomas knew he should have allowed himself to be taken too. I think he knew he should have accompanied Jesus to the cross. But he didn't do what he knew he ought to. He went along with the others. He saved his own skin. And then he couldn't stand himself. Having the type of personality he had, he just wanted to be alone when he'd failed. He was angry at himself, so he was off suffering alone when Jesus returned from the dead to reveal himself. And he missed out on something wonderful.

But the disciples didn't want Thomas to stay down in the dumps. They sought him out to tell him about the Lord's miraculous arising: "We have seen the Lord!" They kept on saying it over and over again. They were all singing the same song. But Thomas's response was disbelief.

That's Thomas for you. Peter said, "Hey, guess what? We saw Jesus!" Simon exclaimed, "Thomas, you missed it! We saw the Lord!" John cried, "He's alive!" Nathanael, Matthew, Andrew—they all delivered the same message. But Thomas was entrenched in doubt.

The Lord understood that John would believe merely on examining shreds of evidence. He knew that Mary's love was all-encompassing, that she'd be wrung through the wringer before the triumph became real to her. He knew she'd have to see him alive before she rebounded from the trauma of watching him die. And Jesus realized that Thomas would have to be confronted with flesh-and-blood proof before he could believe.

Thomas voiced three conditions, before he would believe. He must:

—see the imprint of the nails in the Lord's hands,
—touch the imprint of the nails,
—place his finger in the Lord's wounded side.

That was his list of demands. Look at what the Lord did when he appeared to Thomas eight days later. Just as he called Mary by name at the tomb, so he directly addressed the very items Thomas had mentioned. With another "Peace be with you," the Lord appeared in the midst of the men who a week later had once again gathered behind closed doors.

Did all eyes focus on Thomas, the unconvinced one? It must have been hard for them not to say, "I told you so!" But they loved him, and kept silent in expectation. The Lord looked at the doubting disciple and simply said, "Reach here your finger, and see My hands; reach here your hand, and put it into My side; and be not unbelieving, but believing" (John 20:27 NASB).

See my hands.
Reach with your finger and touch them.
Put your hand into my side.
Believe.

I suspect that Thomas never extended his hand. I think tears must have begun to roll down his cheeks, and probably down the faces of the ten other men as they watched a skeptic come to faith. It is another tender, beautiful scene. "My Lord and my God!" Thomas gasped. He leaped from initial unbelief to total commitment. The intensity of the moment overwhelmed him. The evidence is inescapable. You can touch it. You can handle it. You can see it.

For us, the events are invisible, historical, past tense, but that in no way nullifies their reality. Having watched hundreds over my years of ministry come to Jesus in faith, I know that my redeemer lives and that he is still saving and changing lives. Thomas knew it too.

But Why?

We've seen the responses of John, Mary, Thomas, and the rest of the disciples to the resurrection of Jesus. The reason the Lord included it all in his word is given in verses 30-31 of John 20:

> Many other signs therefore Jesus also performed in the presence of the disciples, which are not written in this book; but these have been written that you may believe that Jesus is the Christ, the Son of God, and that believing you may have life in His name (NASB).

You see, the miracles we've witnessed so far are a drop in the bucket. There were weeks more in which the resurrected Jesus Christ walked the earth. He spent time with the eleven he loved but also with others, including two on the road to the town of Emmaus whom we'll meet in the next chapter. All of it has a purpose: that we might believe that Jesus is the Christ, and therefore have life in his name. Abundant life, now and forever.

Yet we continue to take the cross and the resurrection lightly, when legitimately we shouldn't even consider it without tears streaming down our faces, grateful hearts overflowing with love, minds lifted upward in meditation on him. Scaled eyes, calloused hearts, and lukewarm affections keep us from experiencing the intensity of emotion that should well up in our hearts.

Beyond the Cross

How it must grieve God when we discount the death and arising of his beloved Son. Our response should be like Martin Luther's. It is said that one day a servant knocked on the door of Luther's study. Receiving no answer, he burst in and saw the great theologian prostrate before a crucifix. Not worshiping the object, Luther cried unapologetically as he concentrated on the savior and the sacrifice: "The cross, the cross . . . for me, for me!"

Do you want to know something of how God must feel when we turn our backs on him and refuse to recognize his Son's death and resurrection? A story first printed in *The King's Business* magazine and later reprinted in *Our Daily Bread* spoke to me about the Father's feelings as nothing else has.

While lying in his boat one evening, a Christian fisherman heard a loud splash. He knew that the man in a nearby yacht had been drinking heavily, so without hesitation he dove into the frigid water and managed to pull the half-drowned victim on board the yacht. The Christian administered artificial respiration and placed the man on his berth, going to great pains to make him comfortable. Then he swam back to his own boat. The next morning the fisherman returned to the yacht to see how the man he had saved was doing.

"None of your business!" the fellow snapped defensively.

When the fisherman reminded him that he had saved the man from drowning the night before, the ungrateful fellow cursed him. So the Christian rowed away, tears filling his eyes, the rejection and lack of gratitude stinging him. Then he realized something that made the experience a lesson never to be forgotten. Looking to the heavens, he said in prayer to the Lord, "When I think of how men have treated you, dear Lord, I'm filled with sorrow. Now I can begin to understand just a little how you must feel."

Reflections for the season

1. Is there an area in your life where you are trusting in the natural instead of hoping in the supernatural power of a loving, sovereign God? Determine right now to turn it over to him. Wait, and watch him work.

2. Do you know a doubting Thomas? If you're not already doing it, make a commitment to pray weekly for the salvation of this lost friend or loved one. Perhaps this Easter the Christ will become real to your Thomas.

3. Have you been treating someone in your life the way the disciples did the women who told them about the empty tomb? Have you been throwing buckets of water on the spiritual enthusiasm of someone else? If the answer is yes, ask God to light a fire under you so that instead of quenching the enthusiasm, you'll catch it.

C H A P T E R S E V E N

To Emmaus and Back

Luke 24:13-36

There's an old saying about Texas weather—if you don't like it, wait around an hour; it'll change. And it's true. In the twenty-two years we've been Texans, I can't begin to count the number of times that thick, black, choking clouds pouring rain have suddenly parted to reveal a brilliance of blue sky and sunlight. It's as if the faucets of heaven flow freely in full force, and then are instantly shut off. Soon all that remains of the genuine Texas gully-washer are steamy puddles, stalled cars, and topsoil deposits in the streets.

Down here it's not unusual for a December day to start off in the thirties, and warm up to the seventies before sunset. Texas residents experience no more than three or four hard freezes per year, depending on the section of the state in which they live. Snow pelts the Dallas area once or twice annually, and covers ground in the Panhandle a few times more than that. That's the norm, but 1985 was different.

Nineteen eighty-five blew in with storms that devastated the Rio Grande valley citrus industry. San Antonio and the nearby hill country were blanketed with over a foot of snow. Our capital, Austin, like other central Texas cities, shut down completely. Stores, schools, and offices closed, while everyone played in the crunchy white stuff. Now, I know to some of you reading this, shutting down a city for a foot of snow sounds silly, but we can't even buy snow tires down here. Our cities don't own snowplowing equipment. We deal with icy overpasses by spreading a little salt and sand on them. It's all we can do. So a foot of snow slows us down considerably. Besides, it's safer if we stay inside, because many of us don't know how to drive under snowy, icy conditions anyway. Thin layers of road ice cause drivers down here literally to hit the skids, slip into drainage ditches, and slide across intersections in record numbers.

My point in telling you about our mild winters is not meant to be a tourist spiel for the Lone Star State. I am not being paid by real estate agents to plug the climate. The reason I've told you about the frosty winter of '85 is so I can also tell you about the beautiful spring that same year. Our state is known for its wildflowers. Each year near Easter, bluebonnets burst forth and form azure seas in fields and valleys, coating the countryside. Patches of Indian paintbrush, clover, and other wildflowers also lend color to the landscape. Even our highway medians and the stretches next to the shoulders are covered with flowers: the state highway department has seeded them ever since Lady Bird Johnson called on our nation to spruce things up.

Spring 1985 was a splendid one for wildflower fans. Unusually vast oceans of bluebonnets filled stretches of open land; other flowers sprang up in unaccustomed abundance. Why? We had the snow to thank. The abnormally hard freeze created the conditions for the sprouting of scores of budding plants. Icy, frozen ground thaws to produce the most vivid and largest number of flowers. If it doesn't freeze hard a few times during the winter, we know that the bluebonnets won't be much to look at, come spring. An icy death of sorts must take place before new life will flower to its greatest fullness.

Every spring is much like a resurrection, the dead ground giving way to life. Nature speaks of resurrection in other ways too. We prune rose bushes each February, cutting them back severely so they'll bud and blossom in the warmer months. An acorn is loosened from an oak tree and falls to the ground, where it dries up and, if not eaten by a squirrel, is covered by dirt and dust. Rain falls and seasons change. Soon a tiny shoot appears, green at first, then gradually thickening as the weeks go by. Eventually we have another oak seedling.

Nature speaks of resurrection.

It's one way God's creation tells us about God.

Paul mentioned this in Romans 1:20, where he explained that even those people who have never heard the good news of Jesus Christ have no excuse for failing to respond to God, since God makes himself known in the world he has created:

> For since the creation of the world His invisible attributes, His eternal power and divine nature, have been clearly seen, being understood through what has been made, so that they are without excuse (Romans 1:20 NASB).

What is known about God can be discovered by looking at his universe: the movements of the planets; the sun, moon, and stars; the satellites, seasons, and tides. With its various components and creatures and climates, our planet is a living illustration, an object lesson of resurrection. Why resurrection? It's because God himself, in the person of Jesus Christ, was resurrected. Why shouldn't his creation proclaim it?

The Best Part of the Story

One of the most heartwarming stories about the resurrection of Jesus was told by the late Will A. Houghton. Houghton describes an old gentleman walking down a small-town street, who paused to look at a crucifixion scene in a shopkeeper's window. A small boy stood beside him, also studying the scene. The elderly man didn't appear to notice the little nipper, but then the boy spoke.

"Them's Roman soldiers," the little fellow piped up. The old gentleman said nothing and continued to look.

"There's Jesus," said the lad. Still no comment from the man.

"They killed him," the boy continued. At this, having satisfied his curiosity, the gentleman began to walk away. Behind him he heard the patter of small feet, and the lad caught him by the sleeve and tugged at it.

"Mister!" he exclaimed with urgency. "Wait! I forgot to tell you the most important part! He is alive again!"

The boy had it right, didn't he?

Resurrection is the most important part.

Luke the Physician

So far we've looked at several accounts of eyewitness reports of the resurrection. Now we're about to examine another, from the gospel of Luke.

Luke was a gentile physician, and judging from the compassion with which he wrote, he must have had a terrific bedside manner. He understood people, and described them with homespun honesty, humor, and warmth. Reading the two books of the Bible he wrote—his gospel and the book of Acts, the history of the early church—we get a sense of Luke as one of us, just plain folks, an ordinary man recording extraordinary events. Luke was the gospel writer who most clearly presented Christ's humanity, although he made it clear that Jesus is *God* and man.

Something else about Luke—he never saw the resurrected Christ. He was not an apostle, one of the original twelve disciples chosen by our Lord to be the first ministers of his good news. They were the sent ones. Unlike Peter, John, James, Andrew, and the rest of the crew (including Paul, who was confronted by the living Jesus on the Damascus road after the Lord's ascension, and thereby qualified for apostleship), Luke never saw Jesus in the flesh. He never touched him, never embraced him, never ate with him, never listened to him teach a Bible class. Luke probably became a believer through hearing about Jesus from another, perhaps Paul, whose company he joined at Troas to sail to the region of Macedonia (Acts 16:10-11). But once he became a Christian, Luke's heart burned for the Lord. He longed to tell others about the savior. He lived to evangelize, to spread the good news.

Think how significant it is that Dr. Luke never saw the risen savior, and yet lived for him. In that, he was a lot like you and me, wasn't he? As a scientific man, a practical man, a medical doctor, Luke wouldn't have been likely to believe in myths. Don't you imagine he pored over the evidence with a critical eye? Don't you suppose he examined each shred of the account of Christ with meticulous care? Don't you think he cross-examined the witnesses until there was not even a shadow of doubt in his mind? Surely he didn't rest until he was completely satisfied that the resurrection was real and that Jesus Christ was indeed the promised Jewish messiah.

We can do what Luke did. We can dissect the evidence, and one of the purposes of this book is to help you do just that. In the end, I am convinced that each of us will have no legitimate response except to cry, as Thomas did of Christ, "My Lord and my God!"

Let's turn to Luke's version of the resurrection, realizing as we do that even secular scholars and historians credit him with being an accurate chronicler of the age in which he lived. We'll view one of the most endearing and human accounts of Christ's appearing to those he loved, to some people who, like Luke and us, are just ordinary people.

Setting the Stage

As our scene opens, it was still Easter Sunday. The Lord had already revealed himself to Mary Magdalene at the tomb and to the women on the road back into Jerusalem. Peter and John had seen the discarded grave clothes. Jesus hadn't as yet appeared for the first time to the ten disciples as a group; in fact the men had dismissed the women's reports as nonsense. Evidently the two people we're about to meet knew about the women's experience, although they were not convinced that it really happened. Thoughts of sorrow and regret were probably running through the minds of the pair as they exited the city of Jerusalem to head back home to Emmaus, a town some seven miles away.

Their names? One, the one who talked the most, was Cleopas. The other was a friend, possibly his wife. Probably they were Jews who had come, like multitudes of others who gathered in Jerusalem, to observe the Passover.

Cleopas and the other disciple were different from most of the people assembled in the city to celebrate Passover; they were dedicated followers of Jesus Christ. They had seen his miracles; they were convinced he was the messiah. As the awful events of the week transpired, they listened closely to each report with sinking stomachs, worried brows, and sickened souls. When it apparently was all over, the teacher unjustly dead, their hearts were pierced by grief. We find out about them as we turn to Luke 24. The scripture verses from the passage used below are from my personal translation of the Greek text.

The Appearance—Luke 24:13-16

> And behold, two of them on that very day were going on their way to a village which was about seven miles from Jerusalem; its name, Emmaus. And they were conversing with each other about all these things which had happened. And it came about that while they were conversing and discussing, Jesus himself approached and was walking along with them. But their eyes were being restrained from recognizing him.

According to Luke 24, it was soon after the assembled disciples disparagingly greeted the women's reports of the empty tomb that these two left the big city and headed for the village of Emmaus. Luke doesn't even introduce them to us by name at first. We read simply that "two of them on that very day were going on their way to a village" (24:13).

Isn't it interesting that on this first Easter Sunday, the Lord chose to appear to two virtual nobodies? This pair heading to Emmaus weren't from his inner circle. There was no Emmaus Evangelism Society, no Save the Messiah League of Emmaus. Neither traveler had been healed by the Lord, so far as we know. Neither figures prominently in any of his miracles, that we can tell. Maybe they were among the five thousand fed that day in Judea, but we don't know that. So average were these two that Luke doesn't identify either of them until six verses later, and then we meet only one by name.

And where does this divine revelation take place? Read the text. It's on a dusty little road, on the way to an insignificant little town. If I were Jesus, having been unjustly condemned and executed, I'd have manifested myself first to Caiaphas and then to Pilate. "See there!" I'd exclaim. "You guys just thought you could kill me. I'm back! Try that on for size!"

But not the Lord.

Often in scripture we read of the Lord's revealing himself in the most unlikely of places, to the most unlikely of people. The no-names weren't no-names to him. He called an unimportant sheepmaster named Abram out of a one-horse town called Ur, renamed him Abraham, and you know the rest. He instructed his prophet Samuel to pluck a young whippersnapper named David from among the several sons of Jesse, and to anoint him king of Israel. He chose fishermen to be his closest earthly associates. He appeared to such otherwise unknowns as Micah, Hosea, Amos, and Malachi, and gave them glimpses of the future. God has a way of making nobodies into somebodies.

Here on the road to Emmaus we meet two persons a lot like you and I. They've probably never won a contest. Their names won't be in the newspapers, unless they show up in the vital statistics. Sunday afternoon rolled around and they'd had all they could stand of city life, all they could handle of heartbreak, so they headed out. They loved the Lord Jesus—and he was dead. It was time to turn out the lights. The party was over. The game had ended, and the score was nothing to write home about.

Dejected, the two were "conversing with each other about all these things that had happened" (Luke 24:14). They were hashing and rehashing the week's horrendous happenings. Imagine what they were saying.

"I can't believe he's dead!"

"If only we'd more aggressively defended him!"

"He was so young."

"He never did anybody any harm. Why did people hate him so?"

"You know, if he just hadn't made so many waves. He never was very diplomatic with the Pharisees. He always spoke his mind."

"So? Since when is that a crime? If we'd just been more courageous, none of this would have happened. If we'd spoken out when we should have, they'd have realized there are more of us in the silent majority who really believe in him than they thought."

"It doesn't matter now. He's gone."

Oblivious to the afternoon sunshine, they glumly conversed, mentally kicking themselves for not doing more. We read that "it came about while they were conversing and discussing, Jesus himself approached and was walking along with them" (Luke 24:15). From the rear the savior neared, walking in his resurrected body. Mark 16:12 says of this occasion that the Lord appeared in "a different form" (NASB) than in previous revelations.

Walking beside *us* as he did with the Emmaus disciples—what a great place for God to be. If we let God do for us what he desires to, he'll be walking with us through the rest of this life. He craved fellowship with Adam and Eve, and came down to walk with them in the cool of the day in the garden (see Genesis 3:8-9). He snatched home one man who walked with him, enabling Enoch to bypass physical death. In the person of the Lord Jesus, he chose the twelve to be with him.

God loves to be with you and me too. He longs to communicate with us regularly through his written word and through prayer. But he'll never force the issue. He'll always give us free will, and he's delighted by the heart that freely wills to respond to him.

The risen Christ walked up to the pair on the Emmaus road, and they did not know him for who he was. Luke tells us that their "eyes were being restrained from recognizing him" (24:16). They were blinded to his identity.

Many times in scripture we read of instances in which an individual's vision is restrained. Sometimes even physical blindness results, as in the episode with Elisha and the Arameans, and Paul and the evil magician Elymas (2 Kings 6:17-18; Acts 13:11). We find that sometimes hearts are restrained. Pharaoh's was hardened even as Moses implored him to let the Israelites go (Exodus 7:13). Minds are restrained. The patriarch Joseph's own brothers did not recognize him when they encountered him in Egypt, some twenty-two years after betraying him and selling him into slavery (see Genesis 42:8). The ruler of this present world, Satan, acts to blind the eyes of men and women spiritually to the truth of the gospel (2 Corinthians 4:4).

In the case of the pair on the road to Emmaus, the great restrainer of vision, heart, and mind was the Holy Spirit. He did not yet indwell the Emmaus disciples; that would not happen, remember, until the day of Pentecost. Neither did he come upon them to reveal the identity of the person now walking alongside them. Not yet, anyway.

What about you? As we discussed in chapter 5, one of the functions of the Holy Spirit in the life of a Christian is to illumine, to make clear and comprehensible, the holy scriptures. To put it bluntly, if you're not a believer, it will be tough for you to understand much of the Bible. Maybe a preacher with a gift for communicating will be able to make some of the scripture less fuzzy to you. And surely you'll be able to understand God's hatred of your sin and his plan for the salvation of your soul. But the spiritual spark won't be there to ignite the rest of the word until you choose to believe. "But a natural man does not accept the things of the Spirit of God; for they are foolishness to him, and he cannot understand them, because they are spiritually appraised," wrote Paul (1 Corinthians 2:14 NASB). "Open my eyes that I may see wonderful things in your law," the psalmist implored of the Father (Psalm 119:18 NIV). Only after salvation and the indwelling of the Spirit is the camera lens of your heart in focus.

Eyes blinded, vision restrained, hearts held back until commitment is made—we see it all, even in the twelve. In the upper room Philip said to Jesus, "Lord, show us the Father, and it is enough for us." Jesus' reply? "Have I been so long with you, and yet you have not come to know Me, Philip? He who has seen Me has seen the Father" (John 14:8-9 NASB). Aren't we like Philip? Many times along life's pathway the Lord is right there with us. He speaks to us in a sermon, with a springtime, through a friend, on a freeway, by an illness, with a trauma, or through some other circumstance. Often we're too busy to see his hand. We miss his blessing. We choose blindness over brightness, and great is the tragedy when we do.

As believers, when we walk out of fellowship with the Lord, we walk in the darkness, accompanied by a grieved and quenched Spirit. Growth is paralyzed. Evidences of blessing are gone as we are left to our own devices. Right now two friends of mine, professing Christians, have opted for the darkness of departed glory. They have left their wives and children for other women. But what seemed great at the time has become as bitter as wormwood.

Blindness over brightness—it's pictured in the desperation of two persons walking along a dusty road, lost in loneliness, failing to see that the greatest friend of all time had joined them.

The Problem—Luke 24:17-24

> And he said to them, "What are these words which you are exchanging with each other as you are walking?"
>
> And they stood still looking sad. And one of them named Cleopas answered and said to him, "Are you the only one visiting Jerusalem and unaware of the things that have happened here in these days?"
>
> And he said to them, "What things?"
>
> And they said to him, "The things concerning Jesus the Nazarene, who was a man, a prophet; mighty in deed and word in the sight of God and all the people. And how the chief priests and our rulers delivered him up to a sentence of death and crucified him. But as for us, we were hoping that he himself was about to be liberating Israel. Indeed, besides all this, it is the third day since these things happened. But also, some women among us amazed us when they were at the tomb early in the morning, And not having found his body, they came saying that they had also seen a vision of angels who said that he was living. And some of these with us went to the tomb and found it just exactly as the women also had said; but him they did not see."

Jesus arrived on the scene and desired to be caught up in the two disciples' conversation, so he broke the ice with a simple question, "What are these words which you are exchanging with each other as you are walking?" (Luke 24:17). The two travelers paused and stood still, "looking sad." Christ's question interrupted the flow of the conversation, and also caused the disciples to stop and pay attention to him. Surely everyone had heard about what happened to Jesus. How could this fellow have missed it?

"Are you the only one visiting Jerusalem and unaware of the things that have happened here in these days?" asked one of them named Cleopas (24:18).

"What things?" replied the Lord, probably more than a little amused (Luke 24:19).

To Cleopas and his companion, it seemed that the tragic events of the past week ought to be common knowledge. They had a point. Certainly the news had spread speedily along the Jerusalem grapevine. But in their incredulity, the two were also showing us some very human qualities. When we're going through grief, we often feel that the whole world knows about it. We mourn the loss of a parent or brother or spouse, and we somehow believe that everyone shares our sorrow. How surprised we are when, months after a tragedy, somebody out of the blue inquires about the health of our departed loved one. How amazed we are that they hadn't heard the news. That was the attitude of Cleopas and his friend.

What things had happened in Jerusalem lately? Cleopas and his fellow traveler gave the news to their evidently ignorant new companion. The detail with which Luke records the conversation that follows makes me think that the good doctor probably interviewed Cleopas. It reads much like an accurate news report or court testimony, a collection of "just the facts," as *Dragnet's* Joe Friday would have said. Let's look at the information Cleopas and friend delivered.

"What Things?"

The things concerning Jesus the Nazarene, who was a man, a prophet; mighty in deed and word in the sight of God and all the people (Luke 24:19). In their sorrow, the two spoke in the past tense. This Jesus, who *was* a man, is dead. Cleopas and friend were just as human as you and I; they couldn't see beyond the grave. Jesus was a great man, a great prophet, a mighty servant of God, and now he was gone. That's all they knew.

And how the chief priests and our rulers delivered him up to a sentence of death and crucified him (Luke 24:20). Turning from their picture of the Lord's life, the Emmaus disciples described his death. They blamed their own rulers and the religious establishment.

But as for us, we were hoping that he himself was about to be liberating Israel. Indeed, besides all this, it is the third day since these things happened (Luke 24:21). In other words, why were they feeling so sad about it all? We *were* hoping (past tense) that the one crucified was going to free Israel from Roman domination. We thought we'd seen our earthly king. And then our own chief priests put an end to it all. We even waited around three days. Jesus had said something about coming back to life in three days. Now it's nearly evening, and it just can't be true.

Their expectations had grown ice cold, their enthusiasm completely quenched. There was no gladness in their tone. We loved him. He meant well. But he didn't succeed.

They didn't understand the big picture, did they? No wonder Jesus chose to walk with them. The flame on the altar of their hearts was nearly extinguished. He came to rekindle it. He came to set them ablaze for him. How great to know that we can expect the Lord to make himself known to us in times like these, when all seems black. We've only to be sensitive to his presence and the still small voice saying, "This is the way; walk ye in it."

But also, some women among us amazed us when they were at the tomb early in the morning (Luke 24:22). Cleopas and his companion continued talking. It seems there was an update. There had been a news flash from some women, although it was a bit too much to swallow. Some strange and wonderful stories circulated. Rumors ran rampant.

And not having found his body, they came saying that they had also seen a vision of angels who said that he was living (Luke 24:23). The news flash? The women found an empty tomb and heard angels say the Christ had arisen.

And some of those with us went to the tomb and found it just exactly as the women also had said; but him they did not see (Luke 24:24). So much for the news flash. The update of the women was a washout, according to Cleopas. His words resounded with doubt, ringing with disbelief. The tomb was empty all right, but there was no sign of Jesus. Like Thomas, these two weren't going to believe the Lord was alive until they saw him for themselves.

Little did they know that he was already right there.

I know hundreds of people like Cleopas and his companion. Bound in their unbelief, such folks can't see Christ on a gorgeous Easter morning. He isn't real to them. The empty tomb isn't enough for them. They've got to see him to believe him. They crowd our churches every Easter. Dressed in their finest, looking at lilies, singing the songs, examining the traditions, they may ask themselves: Does anybody really believe this? The truth is shrouded in myth and mystery, as far as their minds can comprehend. They turn away and miss it all, skeptics to the very last chorus of "Christ Arose."

Bible Class—Luke 24:25-27

> And he said to them, "O unintelligent and slow of heart to be believing in all the things which the prophets have spoken. Was it not necessary for the Christ to suffer these things and to enter into his glory?" And beginning from Moses and from all the prophets, he explained to them in all the scriptures the things concerning himself.

Did Jesus turn on them in anger? Did he shake his head and write them off as hopeless, unreachable, unteachable? Did he send them away unsatisfied? Not the Lord.

"Then you will call upon me and come and pray to me, and I will listen to you," the Lord says to his people through the prophet (Jeremiah 29:12-13 NIV). On the Emmaus road the risen Christ turned to Cleopas and his companion, and (I imagine heaving a sigh) said, "O unintelligent and slow of heart to be believing in all the things which the prophets have spoken" (Luke 24:25). It was not a statement made contemptuously or sarcastically. Jesus was not saying, "You stupid fools! You wouldn't know the savior if he walked right up to you!" No, the Lord was speaking in love, and his tone was one of gentle dismay. The travelers had somehow spiritually missed the point. They were so wrapped up in their expectations that they'd forgotten to consult prophetic scripture for an accurate picture of a savior they were convinced was dead. They were slow on the uptake, unaware of the truth, unappraised of the facts. Their ignorance would be short-lived.

"Was it not necessary for the Christ to suffer these things and to enter into his glory?" the Lord continued (Luke 24:26). The messiah was born to die.

These two pilgrims had one enormous problem to overcome as they dealt with the events of the week past. You might say it was the major problem of their generation in accepting Jesus Christ for who he was, the Son of God. The two Emmaus disciples, like just about every other faithful Jewish man and woman two thousand years ago, looked for the coming of a king who would be the savior of their nation, and who would set up a kingdom. They understood the *king* part, but they couldn't comprehend the fact that their king was first going to suffer.

Let's go over that once more. Cleopas and his generation accepted the concept of a coming king, but they rejected the idea of his suffering. What about us today, twenty centuries later? We're not in the same rut as the Jews of Jesus' day, are we? We've come to grips with the suffering part, haven't we? Even atheists and agnostics admit that a man called Jesus died two thousand years ago. We believers accept the idea of a suffering Christ, a savior who loved us enough to hang from a cross. But what about the concept of that suffering savior as a king? Do we endure this life with the expectancy that he is going to come again as a king and set up his messianic kingdom? Do we truly believe it? Is the idea of Jesus as coming king of kings and Lord of lords, real to us? Sadly, I think that often it's not. We can handle the suffering part; it's the kingdom we can't come to grips with. As the Lord looks down, how much we must remind him of Cleopas and friend, trudging along the road, slow of heart and thick of skull.

But Jesus won't let us stay ignorant, if we're honest seekers like the Emmaus disciples. He's given us a picture of the future kingdom in the Bible. It's there for the reading. As for Cleopas and friend, they weren't allowed to stay in the dark either. Luke told us that Jesus, "beginning from Moses and from all the prophets . . . explained to them in all the scriptures the things concerning himself" (24:27).

What a Bible class! I'd give anything to have been there, wouldn't you? I wish they'd had cassette recorders back then; better yet, video cameras and VCRs. The risen Christ walked along and expounded Old Testament christology, starting with the books of Moses: Genesis, Exodus, Leviticus, Numbers, Deuteronomy. He finished Moses' writings and dove headlong into explanations of the revelations of the prophets. Never before or since has there been a better teacher, a better school, more excited students.

I'd be jealous, except for the realization that when we get to eternity, the Lord will give us such a Bible class too. He'll unfold the mysteries of his word. No longer will we see through a glass darkly, as Paul says, but we'll know it all face to face (1 Corinthians 13:12). We'll see how the whole history of the world fits together, how God's perfect plan for our lives is an incredibly beautiful tapestry into which every thread is flawlessly woven. Just imagining it makes me gung-ho for glory! What about you?

What did the Lord tell these two travelers to Emmaus about himself? We do not know for sure, but we can speculate. I imagine he started with Genesis 3:15, where he was first promised to Eve. He continued with the patriarchs of his chosen people. He showed himself as the star of Jacob, the lion of the tribe of Judah, the perfect judge, the sustainer of David, the voice of the psalms, the wisdom behind the proverbs. He plunged into the writings of the prophets, revealing himself as the virgin's son and the suffering servant of Isaiah, the branch of righteousness of Jeremiah, the "plant of renown" of Ezekiel, the cut-out stone of Daniel, the growing lily of Hosea, the hope of Joel, the plowman of Amos, the deliverer of Obadiah. He explained how he was prefigured in Joseph's struggles, Jonah's trials, Job's sufferings. He showed how he was pictured in the prophets. Prophet, priest, and king, he was the Son of David, come to sit on his Father's throne. The tabernacle, the sacrifice, the lamb, the deliverer, the kinsman-redeemer—all those concepts meshed as never before.

All that is but an overview, some guesses as to the content of the Bible study. I'm sure the Lord got specific. He quoted scripture after scripture. He is its author, after all. Besides, there's a lot to quote. The Old Testament contains over three hundred prophetic references to the messiah that were tangibly fulfilled in Jesus Christ. Centuries before the fact, the place and manner of his birth were there for all to see. (Genesis 3:15; Micah 5:2). The coming of the wise men bearing gifts was no secret either (Psalm 72:10; Isaiah 60:6). The Lord's family tree was given (Psalm 2:7; Genesis 21:12; 22:18; 35:10-12; 49:10; Isaiah 11:1; Jeremiah 23:5). His virgin birth was predicted in Isaiah 7:14, his ministry of miracles in Isaiah 35:5-6, his triumphal entry into the city of Jerusalem in Zechariah 9:9. And those are only a few of the Old Testament prophecies fulfilled in his birth and life.

What about the Lord's death and resurrection? I'm quite certain he spared his companions no details about those twists of the plot either. We've looked at several of these prophecies in earlier chapters, yet a simple chart of them might be useful. Looking at the fulfilled prophetic word in black and white ought to make us fall to our knees in amazement and awe. For a more complete look at the prophecies fulfilled in Christ Jesus, I heartily recommend Josh McDowell's *Evidence That Demands a Verdict.* It's a must for the library of every informed Christian. For now, here's a brief look at the prophetic word made complete in the living word, the savior himself.

Prophecies Fulfilled in Jesus' Death and Resurrection

Jesus Betrayed by Judas

Old Testament Prophecy	*New Testament Fulfillment*
Psalm 41:9; 55:12-14	*Matthew 10:4; 26:49-50; John 13:21*

Even my close friend, whom I trusted, he who shared my bread, has lifted up his heel against me (Psalm 41:9 NIV).

Jesus Deserted by his Disciples

Old Testament Prophecy	*New Testament Fulfillment*
Zechariah 13:7	*Mark 14:27,50; Matthew 26:31*

Strike the shepherd, and the sheep will be scattered (Zechariah 13:7b NIV).

Christ's Silence before His Accusers

Old Testament Prophecy	*New Testament Fulfillment*
Isaiah 53:7	*Matthew 27:12-19*

He was oppressed and He was afflicted, Yet He did not open His mouth (Isaiah 53:7a NASB).

Jesus Scourged

Old Testament Prophecy	*New Testament Fulfillment*
Isaiah 53:5; Zechariah 13:6	*Matthew 27:26*

The chastening for our well-being fell upon Him, And by His scourging we are healed (Isaiah 53:5b NASB).

Christ Shamed and Spit Upon

Old Testament Prophecy	*New Testament Fulfillment*
Isaiah 50:6	*Matthew 26:67; Luke 22:63*

I offered my back to those who beat me, my cheeks to those who pulled out my beard; I did not hide my face from mocking and spitting (Isaiah 50:6 NIV).

Jesus Mocked

Old Testament Prophecy	*New Testament Fulfillment*
Psalm 22:7-8	*Matthew 27:31*

All who see me mock me; they hurl insults, shaking their heads: "He trusts in the Lord; let the Lord rescue him. Let him deliver him, since he delights in him" (Psalm 22:7-8 NIV).

Christ's Hands and Feet Pierced

Old Testament Prophecy	*New Testament Fulfillment*
Psalm 22:16; Zechariah 12:10	*Luke 23:33; John 20:25*

Dogs have surrounded me; a band of evil men has encircled me, they have pierced my hands and my feet (Psalm 22:16 NIV).

Jesus Crucified alongside Criminals

Old Testament Prophecy	*New Testament Fulfillment*
Isaiah 53:12	*Matthew 27:38; Mark 15:27-28*

Because he poured out his life unto death, and was numbered with the transgressors (Isaiah 53:12b NIV).

Jesus Praying for His Persecutors

Old Testament Prophecy	*New Testament Fulfillment*
Isaiah 53:12	*Luke 23:34*

For he bore the sin of many, and made intercession for the transgressors (Isaiah 53:12c NIV).

Christ Hated without Reason

Old Testament Prophecy	*New Testament Fulfillment*
Psalm 69:4; Isaiah 49:7	*John 15:25*

Those who hate me without reason outnumber the hairs of my head (Psalm 69:4 NIV).

His Garments Divided and Gambled For

Old Testament Prophecy	*New Testament Fulfillment*
Psalm 22:18	*John 19:23-24*

They divide my garments among them and cast lots for my clothing (Psalm 22:18 NIV).

Christ's Thirst from the Cross
The Offer of Vinegar to Drink

Old Testament Prophecy	*New Testament Fulfillment*
Psalm 69:21	*John 19:28-29; Matthew 27:34*

They put gall in my food and gave me vinegar for my thirst (Psalm 69:21 NIV).

Jesus' Bones Unbroken through the Ordeal of Crucifixion

Old Testament Prophecy	*New Testament Fulfillment*
Psalm 34:20	*John 19:33*

He protects all his bones, not one of them will be broken (Psalm 34:20 NIV).

His Side Pierced

Old Testament Prophecy	*New Testament Fulfillment*
Zechariah 12:10	*John 19:34*

They will look upon me, the one they have pierced (Zechariah 12:10b NIV).

Darkness over the Land

Old Testament Prophecy	*New Testament Fulfillment*
Amos 8:9	*Matthew 27:45*

"In that day," declares the Sovereign Lord, "I will make the sun go down at noon and darken the earth in broad daylight" (Amos 8:9 NIV).

Burial in a Wealthy Man's Tomb

Old Testament Prophecy	*New Testament Fulfillment*
Isaiah 53:9	*Matthew 27:57-60*

His grave was assigned to be with wicked men, Yet He was with a rich man in His death (Isaiah 53:9 NASB).

Christ's Resurrection

Old Testament Prophecy	*New Testament Fulfillment*
Psalm 16:10; 30:3; 41:10; 118:17; Hosea 6:2	*Acts 2:31; 13:33; Luke 24:46; Mark 16:6; Matthew 28:6*

For Thou wilt not abandon my soul to Sheol; Neither wilt Thou allow Thy Holy One to undergo decay (Psalm 16:10 NASB).

The Lord's Ascension

Old Testament Prophecy	*New Testament Fulfillment*
Psalm 68:18	*Acts 1:9*

Thou hast ascended on high (Psalm 68:18a NASB).

The Recognition—Luke 24:28-31

> And they drew near the village where they were going, and he acted as though he would go farther. And they urged him strongly, saying, "Stay with us because it is getting toward evening and the day has already declined," and he went in to stay with them.
>
> And it came about that when he had reclined at table with them, having taken the bread, he blessed it; and having broken it, he was giving it to them. And their eyes were opened, and they recognized him and he vanished from their sight.

Seven miles the three companions covered, the shortest seven miles in history. Or so it must have seemed to the two caught up listening to a teacher like no other delivering a message they had not yet grasped. No one had ever synthesized the scriptures like this stranger. They probably were startled as they reached the outskirts of Emmaus. Where had the time gone?

As they came to the village limits, Jesus indicated that he "would go farther" (Luke 24:28). It was not an empty gesture. Jesus lives in an individual's heart because he has been invited there; the Lord never forces himself on anyone. He would not force his company on these two either. He would not presume. Oh, he would really like to go on with them. If they were captivated by his message and excited about who he was, if they really wanted him to stay, he would be happy to oblige. But he would never hang around where he was not wanted.

Cleopas and his companion longed to know more, so they continued to crave the company of this marvelous teacher. The message had gotten to them. The sky was darkening, so they urged Jesus to stay with them for the evening. They arrived at their destination and invited him inside (Luke 24:29).

Notice that the Lord waited for an invitation before entering their home. That's how it is with us too. He awaits an invitation to be our salvation. But he won't be pushy. He's no high-pressure salesman; he knocks, but he'll never break down the door or shove himself inside. Those aren't his methods.

Cleopas and his companion opened the door, and Jesus entered in. When dinner was served, a strange thing happened. Luke told us that when the meal was set in front of them, the Lord picked up the bread and blessed it, then broke it and distributed it. The guest became the host, just like that.

What happened next? Into the minds of these two, whose vision had been restrained, images of days gone by suddenly exploded. Perhaps they saw the five thousand fed with only five loaves and a couple of fish. Maybe they recalled how Peter or Andrew or John had described the Lord's last supper with his special disciples. Whatever the reason, the actions of Jesus struck a chord in their hearts and they finally saw him for who he really was. "Their eyes were opened and they recognized him" (Luke 24:31).

Time spent with the Lord—that's how we learn to see him more clearly too. From fellowship with him comes revelation from him. I've sensed his presence when writing Bible studies on such passages as 2 Corinthians 3:18, Hebrews 12:1-2, and Revelation 7:12-17. In each case, the truths of his word grabbed me with terrific intensity. If we take time to be in his presence, to get to know him, we'll be aware how real and how relevant he is.

What did Jesus do when the Emmaus disciples discovered his identity? He vanished. Time and space did not hold him. He was not bound by human limitations. Because the two travelers finally understood who he was, his work for the moment was done. And so he departed.

The Response—Luke 24:32-36

> And they said to one another, "Was not our heart burning within us as he was talking with us along the road, as he was opening (explaining) the scriptures to us?"
>
> And having arisen that very hour, they returned to Jerusalem and found gathered together the eleven, and those who were with them, saying, "The Lord has really risen and has appeared to Simon." And they were relating their experiences on the road and how he was made known to them by the breaking of the bread. And while they were saying these things, he himself stood in their midst.

When the Lord vanished, the excitement really started. The two stared at each other, then began bubbling over with comments and questions. "Was not our heart burning within us as he was talking with us along the road, opening the scriptures to us?" No wonder we were thrilled by his every syllable! No wonder all that scripture fit together so clearly, like the pieces of a giant jigsaw puzzle! He was the one who fashioned it all in the first place.

Their hearts were burning with excitement, enthusiasm, conviction. The prophet Jeremiah knew all about it. He thought about trying not to speak the word of the Lord anymore, but found holding back impossible.

> But if I say, "I will not mention him
>   or speak any more his name,"
> his word is in my heart like a fire,
>   a fire shut up in my bones.

I am weary of holding it in;
indeed, I cannot (Jeremiah 20:9 NIV).

That kind of heavenly heartburn, heaven-sent eagerness and joy and intensity, comes only when you truly know God. Even when we are Christians though, how easy it is for us, like the church of Ephesus in Revelation, to lose our first love. Like the church of Laodicea, we stay neither hot nor cold, but lapse into lukewarmness. We lack the fervor, fire, passion, devotion, to reach a dying world with the message of Jesus.

It was not the breaking of bread that ignited the Emmaus disciples' hearts. They became enthusiastic about Jesus Christ when they delved deeply into his scripture, when they allowed him to teach them biblical principles, when they truly understood his importance. It was along the road that they began to burn for him. And once they actually saw him, they took off running in their ecstasy.

Where did these two go? They returned to Jerusalem. Seven miles, back the other way. Seven miles, retracing their steps.

Think about it. Day was definitely done . . . and gone the sun. It was evening—night would fall at any minute. The Emmaus disciples could have conjured up a million excuses to stay home. We'll go first thing in the morning. Let's turn in tonight. Traveling after dark along a farm-to-market road is dangerous. There might be muggers, wild animals. We're tired. There are no lights along the way either. The disciples in Jerusalem won't believe us anyway.

Yes, they could have come up with a million excuses. But they didn't.

I'm reminded of the account from 2 Kings 7 of the four lepers starving outside the city gates in wartime. People within the city were going hungry, so the lepers had no hope there. If they stayed where they were, their fate would be the same. So they decided to sneak to the enemy camp. The worst that could happen was they'd be killed, and they were going to starve to death anyway, so what difference did it make? They made it to the camp and found a surprise. It was empty of people and filled with food. They gorged themselves on the goods, and loaded up with silver, gold, and clothes. And then one of them remembered that everyone in the city was still starving while they were stuffing. "We're not doing right," they said among themselves. "This is a day of good news and we are keeping it to ourselves. If we wait until daylight, punishment will overtake us. Let's go at once and report this to the royal palace" (2 Kings 7:9 NIV). And they did. Their excitement superseded their natural selfishness, not to mention their fear of reprisal.

Are you that enthusiastic about the riches the Lord has given you? Are you that excited about your relationship with him? Do thoughts of his return thrill you? Will going to heaven be like going home for you? Are you so filled with him that you're overflowing with desire to tell others about him? Or are you stuck in silence?

How many people whose lives you touch have never heard about Jesus Christ because you won't talk about him? Or because you're not too sure about him yourself? Or because you don't know him too well, so you can't share him with anybody else? How many?

The Emmaus disciples didn't hesitate a moment. They jumped up, left the dirty dishes, forgot about their tiredness, to head for Jerusalem. Probably they arrived about 9:00 p.m. or so, and what did they find? Luke 24:33 says they "found gathered together the eleven, and those who were with them."

The eleven—the name by which the men specially chosen by Jesus to be his closest disciples were now described. They used to be called the twelve, but with Judas's desertion and demise, the designation changed. When a majority of the remaining disciples were gathered together, they were now referred to in scripture as the eleven, whether or not all eleven were actually present (see also Acts 1:26). On this evening the travelers from Emmaus found that only ten of the disciples were there; Thomas was off somewhere. They began, as Luke recorded, "relating their experiences on the road and how he was made known to them by the breaking of the bread" (24:35). Picture the dialogue:

"The Lord is alive! Really!"

"He explained it all, from the writings of Moses and the prophets. He was supposed to die. It's okay!"

"We saw him. He ate with us. You should have seen it. At first we thought, Who is this man? And then we knew!"

"I'll never forget him!"

Everybody couldn't be hallucinating, could they? First Mary and the other women, then Peter, now these two from Emmaus. And do you know what happened next? In the middle of it all, the Lord Jesus made his first appearance to the assembled disciples. He materialized in their midst (Luke 24:36).

The Temperature of Your Heart

When the reality of Jesus Christ was revealed to them, the hearts of the Emmaus disciples burned within them. Their minds longed to know more. Their enthusiasm empowered a quick return trip to Jerusalem. May I take this opportunity to ask *you* what the Lord essentially asked them? What is the temperature of your heart concerning Jesus?

The temperature of your heart—is it cold toward him, lukewarm, or blazing with love and gratitude? Are you feeling that he's discouraged with you? That there's no hope for his forgiveness and blessing? You're wrong. Look at which of the eleven he appeared to first in his resurrected state: Peter. Yes, Simon Peter, who publicly denied Jesus three times. The others, except for John, simply crept away, left the field. Peter fumbled the snap on the most critical play, but the Lord appeared to him first.

The Lord is longing to make himself real to you. He won't suddenly materialize in your presence, because that type of pop-up appearance isn't in his game plan for the present. But he will teach you about himself in his word, and you will feel his presence, strength, and comfort as you talk with him in prayer.

Once you come in contact with the living Lord, you ought not to be the same person. Look at Cleopas. At first he was downtrodden, doubtful, about as far down in the dumps as a person could be. His hopes were shattered, his heart sick. Then Jesus came and changed all that.

To Emmaus and back.

The Lord longs to make the trip with each of us.

Ideas for the Fire

J. B. Phillips translates Romans 12:11 this way, "Let us not allow slackness to spoil our work and let us keep the fires of the spirit burning as we do our work for God."

I like his rendition. But how, practically, can we keep the fires of the Spirit burning within us as we do our work for God? Here are a few suggestions.

To keep burning, we must:

1. *Stay close to the source of the fire*—that is, the living Lord.
2. *Fellowship with others on fire.* It's tough to burn alone; logs close together keep one another ignited. United, we help keep each other aflame.
3. *Be willing to be consumed.* Are we ready to go the distance?

Maybe such thoughts as those above are what Kurt Kaiser had in mind when he composed "Pass It On." Let's not forget that:

It only takes a spark
To get a fire going,

And soon all those around
Can warm up in its glowing;
That's how it is with God's love,
Once you've experienced it:
You spread His love to ev'ryone,
You want to pass it on.

Reflections for the season

1. Two unknown disciples are immortalized in scripture as they walk the Emmaus road and there meet the living Lord. What does this tell you about God's concern for the "little people"?

2. Nature speaks of resurrection in many ways: in the flowers of spring, the cycle of the seasons, the movements of the tides. In what other ways is God's greatest work, the resurrection, made evident in his creation?

3. What is the temperature of your heart today concerning Christ Jesus?

C H A P T E R E I G H T

The Great Cover-Up

Matthew 28:11-20

Madalyn Murray O'Hair—whenever her name is mentioned, it evokes a response. There's no neutrality where Mrs. O'Hair is concerned. Nineteen eighty-nine marks the twenty-fifth anniversary of the Supreme Court decision removing prayer and Bible reading from public schools. As instigator of the original lawsuit, in which her elder son, Bill, was named as plaintiff, O'Hair became a household name in the early '60s. Since then she has continued to challenge the legality of various other "religious" practices in public life. She successfully prevented astronaut Buzz Aldrin from taking a televised communion on the moon. A Texas constitutional provision requiring individuals to express belief in a supreme being before assuming public office is no longer enforced, thanks to O'Hair's litigious spirit. She has also fought tax exemptions for churches and attempted to have the phrase "In God We Trust" removed from U.S. currency, so far to no avail. Once calling herself "the most hated woman in America," Madalyn Murray O'Hair is certainly the best-known professional atheist alive today, and by far the most vocal (Wright, 1989).

Back in the mid '70's, when I was teaching a Bible class at the University of Texas in Austin, I was invited by the political science department to debate O'Hair. Christian friends advised me against doing so, for three reasons: she wouldn't fight fair; she'd focus on emotional issues, not intellectual ones; she'd use a lot of profanity. I declined the invitation, and then was asked to speak the week following O'Hair's address. My topic? The Christian faith. I gladly accepted, and centered my talk on four issues:

1. The existence of God
2. The deity of Christ
3. The inspiration and authority of scripture
4. The validity of the Christian experience

You can fight forever over the first three issues, but no one can argue when I say, "Once I was blind, but now I see." The miracle of the life-changing new birth is far and away the greatest argument for New Testament Christianity (see 2 Corinthians 5:17). Yet skeptics still choose to deny it, as they have for centuries.

Did you know that even the furious phenomenon of a Madalyn Murray O'Hair is nothing new. Hers is not the first vehement challenge of Christianity. She's not the first to deny the existence of God and to decry faith as anti-intellectual. She's not the first to scoff at the divinity of Jesus Christ. She's not the first, and it's likely she'll not be the last either.

It's safe to say that every generation since the cross has had its Madalyn Murray O'Hairs. Did you ever hear of Robert Ingersoll? Your grandparents or great-grandparents probably did. A lawyer, he was the best-known atheist of the nineteenth century. The son of an austere minister who raised his children harshly, Ingersoll and his brother grew up to disdain the God their father supposedly served. An outspoken critic of Christianity, Ingersoll authored volumes arguing against the reality of God and the credibility of Christ. He toured widely, debating Bible scholars and lecturing on reasons for unbelief. Ingersoll often ended such addresses by challenging God to strike him dead within five minutes if the Lord were truly alive. The seconds ticking off made for high drama in the packed auditoriums. Since God never chose to take him up on his offer, Ingersoll always snapped shut his pocketwatch with a smug, satisfied look, and proclaimed that he had proved there obviously was no God. (Hearing of those theatrics, the late London preacher, Dr. Joseph Parker, remarked, "And did the American gentlemen think he could exhaust the patience of God in five minutes?") Like O'Hair to date, there is no record that Ingersoll ever changed his mind about the existence of God. "There will be no singing," read his funeral notices, a cold reminder that because of his resistance and rebellion, there really was nothing to sing about at Ingersoll's death.

Atheists, agnostics, individuals who doubt, deny, and sometimes even fervently try to disprove the existence of God the Father, Son, and Spirit—we'll always have them around as long as the world exists in its present form. Madalyn Murray O'Hair is nothing new. Unless she turns her back on a virtual lifetime of profaning the Lord and genuinely comes to faith in him, her funeral will be nothing to sing about either. I hope and pray that she'll repent and receive the savior; God's arms are open to love and accept her too.

One thing that struck me while reading an article about her recently is that she claims to have read the Bible through, and rejected it as vulgar, sado-masochistic, cruel, and mythic. Because she's an intelligent woman, it is hard to believe she has objectively examined the proofs of Jesus' life, death, resurrection, and ascension. Certainly she can successfully attack the conduct of professing Christians. With the 1980s scandals in televised religion, the church is not only handing her the ammo, we're popping the cartridges into place and parading before her like ducks in a shooting gallery.

Yes, Christians can be criticized, but I do not believe that even one paragraph of the Bible can be successfully contradicted. Embracing Christianity does not mean that one discards intelligent thought. Faith is rational. In fact, when one examines the evidence, faith in Christ is the only logical, intelligent response to the scriptural record.

Christianity makes sense. You're not burying your brain cells when you commit yourself to Christ. The faith you're adopting can be successfully defended.

Think of the Bible itself. No document written over a period of sixteen hundred years by over forty different authors from diverse walks of life, using three languages, could possibly have the continuity and cohesiveness of the holy scripture unless it was inspired by God. The plan of the Lord's redemption of humankind binds the Old and New Testaments together into a remarkable whole. Credible extrabiblical sources such as secular histories and archaeological discoveries consistently confirm the historical and geographical accuracy of scripture. That Jesus Christ was a historical person is indisputable. Flavius Josephus, a Jewish historian and Pharisee born four years after Jesus' death and resurrection, recorded:

> Now, there was about this time Jesus, a wise man, if it be lawful to call him a man, for he was a doer of wonderful works,—a teacher of such men as receive the truth with pleasure. He drew over to him both many of the Jews, and many of the Gentiles. He was Christ; and when Pilate, at the suggestion of the principal men amongst us, had condemned him to the cross, those that loved him at first did not forsake him, for he appeared to them alive again the third day; as the divine prophets had foretold these and ten thousand other wonderful things concerning him; and the tribe of Christians, so named from him, are not extinct at this day (Whiston 379).

Josephus was not the only secular historian of antiquity to chronicle the life of Christ. Others such as Pliny the Younger and Suetonius number among the scores of authors to mention him as a historical person. Indeed, few modern historians deny that Jesus existed in human flesh.

"The poor you will always have with you," Christ once commented (Matthew 26:11 NIV). And we'll also have the doubters, we might add.

But before we go further, let me say that it is not the purpose of this chapter to refute every criticism of the Bible's authenticity, God's existence, and Christ's deity. Volumes have been written to do just that, and for readers desiring to be better informed about the rational basis of their faith, I recommend Paul Little's *Know Why You Believe* and also Josh McDowell's *Evidence that Demands a Verdict*, mentioned in the last chapter.

What I do hope you'll become convinced of as we pore over verses 11-20 of Matthew 28 is the reasonableness of Christ's resurrection. You see, in his day, there were Ingersolls and O'Hairs too. There were skeptics who for their own reasons tried to discredit the resurrection. The empty tomb bred dependence on God in some hearts, a desire to deceive in others. And a great cover-up was concocted to explain away one of the best attested facts in human history: the resurrection of the Christ.

Matthew was writing to convince his mostly Jewish audience that Jesus Christ was king, the promised messiah making a valid offer of the kingdom they longed for, and that he was rejected and crucified. Let's turn to chapter 28 of his book and see some of the first scoffers. Again we'll be using my personal translation of the Greek text.

The Religious Establishment's Reaction—Matthew 28:11-15

> Now while they were going on their way, behold, some of the guard came into the city and reported to the chief priests all that had happened. And when they had assembled with the elders and counseled together, they gave a

> large sum of money to the soldiers, saying, "You are to say, 'His disciples came by night and stole him away while we were sleeping.' And if this should come to the governor's ears, we will win him over and keep you out of trouble." And they took the money and did as they had been instructed; and this story was widely spread among the Jews, and is to this day.

Let's back up in Matthew just a bit to set the stage for this chapter's events. The first seven verses of chapter 28 tell us about the women's early Easter morning excursion to the empty tomb. An earthquake had occurred, the stone in front of the tomb's entrance was rolled away by an angel, the guards had fled, and an angel waited within to give the women the glorious news that the Lord was alive and was planning to see his disciples.

We pick up the action as the guards, frightened because their charge had flown the coop, entered Jerusalem to relate the incredible news to the chief priests. We'll witness how the religious establishment—the Pharisees and Sadducees composing the Jewish governing body or Sanhedrin—dealt with the whole episode. These leaders were the ones with the most to lose materially and socially if this Jesus were truly the messiah. His resurrection would affect their position, pre-eminence, reputation; there would be a new order, a new religion. Much was at stake if this Jesus were the savior, if news that he was alive were allowed to spread.

A Promise of Prosperity—Matthew 28:11-13

Here's the early morning picture. The ground shook with violent tremors; the terror of the guards keeping watch over Jesus' tomb steadily mounted. An angel appeared to roll away the immense stone covering the mouth of the cave, and the tough Roman guards fainted dead away. On awakening and finding the grave vacant, their terror increased at the thought of being accused of dereliction of duty. There was no use guarding an empty tomb, so they took off for town, heading not for their military superiors, but for the Jewish chief priests.

Imagine it.

Close to dawn on this Easter Sunday morning the Roman guards tumbled into town to rouse the religious leaders with their news of trouble. The chief priests and elders held an emergency meeting to discuss what to do. They must nip this thing in the bud. Otherwise the whole world would believe in this charismatic magician, and they'd lose their influence. Matthew recounted that they "counseled together . . . [and] gave a large sum of money to the soldiers" (28:12). In other words they told the soldiers to cover up the truth. It cost them big bucks but it was necessary. The guards could not be allowed to confirm the resurrection, or their religious world would be shattered.

Matthew is the only one of the gospel writers to record this incident of bribery. Why didn't the religious leaders acknowledge their mistake and begin to examine the idea that Jesus might be the messiah? Why did they continue to resist a truth that would be so much easier for them to accept? The fact is that they were unwilling to let the truth penetrate their hearts. They were going to have things their way, live as they had been living, believe what they wanted to believe. Doing that was their prerogative, because God wasn't going to force himself on them, anymore than he forces himself on you, me, or any of us.

By shelling out silver, the scoffers tried to discredit the resurrection. The soldiers assigned to watch over the tomb were the first paid to deny the reason for its emptiness. And why shouldn't they take what they could get out of it? They were not Jews. The sect of Judaism in which people followed this Jesus fellow was nothing to them. They might be in big trouble with their superiors anyway for allowing the tomb to be opened. They'd better go for the gold while they could.

A Necessary Pretense—Matthew 28:13

The Roman guards were expected to *earn* the money paid them under the table. The religious leaders instructed them in what to say when asked about the vacant grave: "His disciples came by night and stole him away while we were sleeping" (Matthew 28:13). There it is—the big lie, the fictional account to be given in exchange for financial reward.

Let's look at the story. The soldiers were to explain that Jesus' disciples robbed the grave of his body while they slept. I can just imagine what their cynical commander might have replied to this. Hmmm, fellows, that's interesting. You mean that the disciples sneaked up to the tomb, broke the seal on the stone, rolled away that gigantic rock from the entrance, all without making a sound? Somehow those disciples, those fishermen, managed a commando raid and you didn't hear a thing? All eleven of them came and snatched the body? Their feet dislodged no pebbles, pressed down no blades of grass, crunched against no sticks? They didn't grunt and groan while heaving the stone out of place? Nobody sneezed? You slept through it all, you say? Well, let me ask you this, then. If you were really sleeping that soundly, how did you know it was the *disciples* who robbed the grave? You didn't see them, did you?

It doesn't take many shots to fill the soldiers' story full of holes, does it? A competent lawyer would make mincemeat of such perjured testimony within minutes of its admission in court. A judge might throw it out.

The soldiers' story held even less water than some of the ones I tried to pull over on my parents while in grade school. I can remember playing with matches one day down near the railroad tracks in a big, grassy field at the end of our block. I was playing hobo, and started a little fire to boil "coffee" in an old tin can. When the fire got away from me, I made a beeline for my upstairs bedroom. Soon sirens were heard and fire engines whizzed by to save the day. I knew I'd be sitting on a burning bottom if I acknowledged my guilt to my father, so when the shakedown later commenced, I concocted some story. Trouble was, my version had enough holes in it to sink a battleship, and we headed for the woodshed anyway. Dad was probably more disappointed over my dishonesty than my carelessness.

Honesty really is the best policy. Too bad the soldiers fogged the issue and blew smoke, instead of coming clean about the empty tomb.

A Pledge of Protection—Matthew 28:14-15

Actually, it was unusual that the Roman soldiers were even involved in the episode. Why were they at a graveyard in the first place? How many times are dead men guarded? The soldiers were stationed at the tomb because the chief priests and leaders feared that the disciples would fake things and make it appear that Jesus had arisen. Matthew 27 records that the religious leaders approached Pilate as early as Saturday morning following the crucifixion with an unusual request. The episode reads as follows:

> Now on the next day, which is the one after the preparation, the chief priests and Pharisees gathered together with Pilate, and said, "Sir, we remember that when He was still alive that deceiver said, 'After three days I am to rise again.' Therefore, give orders for the grave to be made secure until the third day, lest the disciples come and steal Him away and say to the people, 'He has risen from the dead,' and the last deception will be worse than the first." Pilate said to them, "You have a guard; go, make it as secure as you know how." And they went and made the grave secure, and along with the guard, they set a seal on the stone (Matthew 27:62-66 NASB).

The poor Pharisees—as soon as the dead body was lowered from the cross and taken to its tomb, they figured their problems were over. They celebrated their evening meal with joy and relief; they were even giddy with victory. The heretic was dead. Then—I like to think in the middle of the night so their sleep was interrupted—the wheels started spinning again. A terrible thought struck them. Wait a minute! Didn't this Jesus say something about rising again in three days? If his followers faked his resurrection by stealing his body, the Pharisees would be in worse shape than before. Everyone would believe Jesus was the messiah. Something had to be done. As soon as possible the next day they went to find Pilate.

"You have a guard; go, make it as secure as you know how," Pilate replied to their request for help. Some scholars believe that Pilate's answer was not an offer of help, but a statement of fact; that he was not volunteering the services of his Roman soldiers, but instead was telling the Pharisees that they already had their own temple guard, and they should post a Jewish guard at the grave.

Most commentators are convinced, however, that Pilate was referring to a Roman guard. It is mentioned that a seal was fixed to the stone, and this type of sealing was a Roman custom. A cord would be stretched across the stone and sealed on either side by the wax impression of the governor's or a nobleman's signet ring. That way, any tampering with the tomb could be easily detected.

The fact that the guards ran directly to the chief priests on Easter morning, rather than to their own Roman military superiors, might seem to suggest that the guards were Jewish. Why would Romans report to Jews? But it's more likely that the guards ran first to the chief priests because their failure to secure the tomb had placed them in fear for their lives. Roman army discipline was severe. The penalty for dereliction of duty was death, and historical records reveal incidents in which this harsh punishment was meted out (see Acts 12:18-19, for example). Probably the Roman soldiers fled first to the Pharisees in hopes that the Jews could square things with their commanders.

One thing is certain, the guards who kept watch over the grave were nervous about the idea of claiming they were asleep on duty. They didn't accept the bribe from the chief priests until *after* the religious bigwigs guaranteed to protect them. "And if this should come to the governor's ears," the Jewish leaders assured the soldiers, "we will win him over and keep you out of trouble" (Matthew 28:14). That pledge of protection was essential. The soldiers' fear of punishment from the higher-ups suggests strongly they were Romans. Jewish temple guards wouldn't be afraid of the governor's reaction; they were under the jurisdiction of the chief priests, not the secular authorities.

Whatever the case, the guards pocketed the hush money, and did as they were told. Their false version of the resurrection "was widely spread among the Jews, and is to this day" (Matthew 28:15). How right the apostle was. Two thousand years after the fact, the theory that Jesus' body was stolen is still argued.

Rumors spread fast. Mark Twain said that "a lie can go 'round the world, while truth is still lacing up her boots." And lies are long-lived too. "One of the striking differences between a cat and a lie is that the cat has only nine lives," Twain also once observed.

Regrettably, a tendency to believe the unfounded permeates our society, and is a rampant infection gripping even the evangelical church. Our prayer chains, fellowship groups, women's circles, and men's breakfasts are often occasions for dropping tidbits of information about poor Liz or struggling Sid, just enough juicy stuff so we can effectively "pray" for the brother or sister in need. Ron Lee Davis, in *A Forgiving God in an Unforgiving World*, has five suggestions for stopping such idle chatter. Who knows? Maybe if somebody had asked these questions of the Roman soldiers, the story of a stolen body would have been immediately stripped of its effectiveness. Let's look briefly at Davis's keys to checking rumors at the door. When we go head to head with gossip, let's ask these questions:

1. Why are you telling me?
2. Where did you get your information?
3. Have you gone directly to the person you are telling me about and talked to him or her about it?
4. Have you checked out all the facts?
5. Do you mind if I quote you? (Davis 167).

If you haven't guessed, the fifth one is the stopper.

The whole Matthew 27 episode makes me think of how things are going to be after the rapture, the time before the Lord Jesus comes again, when he will snatch his church heavenward. I wonder what the folks who are left behind are going to say about the sudden disappearance of millions of Christians. What excuses will they conjure up? What explanations will they offer? Just hear the speculation. Oh, those religious fanatics have all been kidnapped. The empty graves? The bodies have been stolen, and the other Christians are hiding somewhere. They've found some big cave to hole up in. They're keeping under cover just so we'll think that Jesus fellow called for them. You know, I think it was UFOs. Aliens have grabbed them. That's got to be it.

It's going to take more faith to believe the phony stories of the rapture than to trust the accuracy of the biblical account. Yet I wouldn't put it past the human race to settle for foolishness instead of accepting the scriptural facts at face value. That's what they did in Jesus' day. They settled for the unlikely, the impossible, rather than believing in the power of God to resurrect the dead. When you examine the facts, it is actually anti-intellectual to come to any conclusion about the empty tomb except that Jesus arose. Let's briefly look at some of the most prominent secular theories about what happened at the grave, and you'll see what I mean.

But What If. . . ?

Theory number one: The disciples stole the body while the

guards slept. We've already discussed why this is unlikely. The guards privately admitted that there was no theft. An enormous stone blocked the tomb's entrance; moving it would require great strength and would result in more than enough noise to awaken a sleeping guard detail, especially when the soldiers were threatened with the possibility of death if negligent. Don't forget the fact that the grave clothes remained in the tomb and were seen there by Peter and John, among others. What kind of grave robbers would take the time to unwind the spice-filled linen wrappings and remove the face cloth before carting a body away? Such a time-consuming procedure would only increase their risk of discovery, and they surely didn't want to be caught. Don't forget the appearances of the angelic messengers either. Some might argue that the women were hallucinating, but their delusions were certainly remarkably similar.

Theory number two: The tomb the soldiers guarded was the wrong one. Jesus was never in there. Let's look at this theory, and its variations, such as the idea that Joseph of Arimathea didn't lay the body in his family tomb, but in another grave, and the theory that the women went to the wrong tomb on Easter morning. Who took the soldiers to the tomb in the first place? It was the chief priests and Pharisees. Do you think they went to the wrong one? What about Mary Magdalene and the other women? Mark 15:47 tells us that when Joseph of Arimathea placed Christ's body in the crypt, the women "marked" its location. Were they going to forget something that important so quickly? They saw and took note of where the body was left. Could they have been so befuddled in the early morning that they went to just any old tomb? All four gospels record that Joseph laid Jesus' body in his family crypt (see Matthew 27:57-58; Mark 15:42-45; Luke 23:50-52; John 19:38).

The location of Joseph's tomb was a matter of public record. In those days, people purchased and prepared family burial places long before they were needed. Joseph's rock-hewn sepulcher was known to others; it was no closely guarded family secret. It takes more imagination to believe that some people became confused about the tomb than to believe that Jesus walked out of it alive. Besides, when Mary Magdalene told Peter and John about the empty tomb, they immediately jumped up and began to run there ahead of her. They knew exactly where they were going. They knew precisely where Christ's body was left. They sped to the gravesite and entered to find a discarded shroud. Surely they didn't run to the wrong place too. Those people may have been grieving, but they weren't careless.

Theory number three: Jesus didn't actually die on the cross. He only fainted, or swooned, and appeared dead. Once inside the cool sepulcher, he revived and walked out under his own steam. This suggestion is more fantastic than the others. Do you think Jesus didn't die? Do you want to prove it? Okay, let somebody scourge you, slicing your back open, flaying your flesh with a sharp-tipped cat-o-nine-tails thirty-nine times. Then let some cruel jokester push a crown of thorns down hard on your head till you bleed. Sit calmly while he and his cohorts mock you and spit on you. Carry a heavy wooden cross through the city streets till you can go no farther and collapse under the strain. Let yourself virtually be dragged the rest of the way while someone else bears the cross. Climb a small hill outside Jerusalem and let husky, heartless soldiers throw you across the wooden beams you had carried. Let them pound nails into your hands and feet and fasten you to the cross. Let them hoist the apparatus, with you attached, upward roughly, and carelessly drop it into a hole in the ground. Hang there in the heat for six hours, three in the light and three in darkness, while the world becomes black and the only constant companion you've ever known, your heavenly Father, withdraws his fellowship and leaves you utterly, completely, agonizingly alone. Ask for nothing to drink till it's just about over. At 3:00 p.m., when a Roman soldier comes over to break your legs and thus mercifully hasten your death, convince him that you're already dead. Fool him. He's only witnessed hundreds of executions, maybe thousands, so it ought to be easy. When he doesn't break your legs, you'll know he's certain you're dead. Let one of the soldiers then shove his spear into your side so that blood and water trickle out. Stop your heart from beating while this happens, so that the blood won't spurt or gush, but will be only a stream of coagulating matter accompanied by a watery substance. Let them lower you from the cross. Then let one of your buddies wrap your body tightly in a linen shroud, laying perhaps seventy pounds of spices inside the folds of material, as Joseph of Arimathea probably did. Let him swathe your face in cloth and spices too, so that even if you could breathe, you'd suffocate from the packaging and the strong odor of the aloes and myrrh. Then let your friend place you in a poorly ventilated cave and seal it with an enormous stone and place a guard of Roman soldiers around it.

Let's see you wake up, unwrap yourself, push away the stone undetected, and emerge fit enough to make a seven-mile hike to the town of Emmaus.

If you could do all of that, you'd convince me that Jesus might only have swooned on the cross. And I'd be wondering if maybe I shouldn't be bowing down before you too, because surely it would take supernatural power to effect such a miraculous recovery. Isn't it a lot easier to believe in the resurrection?

Theory number four: Finally, let's say that everyone who thought they saw the resurrected Christ just hallucinated. It was all a mass delusion the likes of which the world hasn't seen since. Maybe it was mass hypnosis. That explains it. Mary, Mary Magdalene, John, Peter, the apostles, the Emmaus disciples, Thomas, five hundred other folks who all saw Jesus at different times—they all hallucinated, right?

Wrong. Different people at different times, from different walks of life, with different personalities and propensities, in different states of mind, saw the risen Christ. We've mentioned his appearances before, but here is a brief list to remind you of the occasions in which Jesus appeared, the first five of which took place on Easter Sunday:

1. To Mary Magdalene, weeping at the tomb
2. To the other women who had visited the grave, as they headed back into the city fearful and astonished
3. To Peter
4. To the disciples on the road to Emmaus
5. To the ten disciples in Jerusalem
6. One week later to the eleven disciples, with Thomas present
7. To seven of the disciples beside the sea of Galilee
8. To over five hundred brethren, including the apostles, in Galilee
9. To James, his half-brother
10. To the disciples on the mount of Olives on the day of ascension
11. To the apostle Paul on the Damascus road

Appointment, Adoration, Agnosticism, and Farewell Address—Matthew 28:16-20

> Now the eleven disciples went on their way to Galilee,to the mountain where Jesus had appointed them. And when they saw him, they worshiped him; but some were doubtful. And Jesus came up and spoke to them, saying, "All authority has been given to me in heaven and on earth. Go therefore and make disciples of all the nations, baptizing them in the name of the Father and the Son and the Holy Spirit, teaching them to observe all that I commanded you; and lo, I am with you all the days, unto the consummation of the age."

The Appointment. While the religious establishment was rejecting the resurrection, and spreading rumors to discredit it, the real disciples of Jesus were busy. They had a meeting to attend, a divine appointment to keep. Remember, the angel told the women at the tomb that Jesus would join his disciples in Galilee (Matthew 28:7). Since then, the Lord had appeared numerous times. One of those appearances is recorded in 1 Corinthians 15:6, where Paul wrote, "After that He appeared to more than five hundred brethren at one time, most of whom remain till now, but some have fallen asleep" (NASB). It is this appearance of the Lord to over five hundred brethren, his disciples included, that I believe is described in the rest of Matthew 28.

In verse 16 we read, "Now the eleven disciples went on their way to Galilee to the mountain where Jesus had appointed them." At first glance, it sounds as if the disciples beat it out of town just after the Roman soldiers began earning their hush money by lying about the empty tomb, but actually the eleven left for Galilee weeks after Easter Sunday. Their rendezvous with the Lord took place sometime between day eight and day forty, at some point after Thomas saw Jesus and stopped doubting, but before the Lord's ascension as recorded in Acts 1:9. Probably in one of his previous appearances, Christ had told his disciples to meet him at a specific place in Galilee at a specific time.

The text suggests, as we'll see in a minute, that the eleven were not the only followers of Jesus to make this journey to Galilee. Others in the city got wind of the disciples' planned departure. Word was out, and by the time the place of rendezvous was reached, over five hundred were in the audience. They wanted to see Jesus too.

Adoration and Agnosticism. We know that more than the eleven were present at this meeting with the Lord because of the response recorded of those who were there. Matthew told us that "when they saw him, they worshiped him; but some were doubtful" (28:17). The coming of the risen king evoked two distinct responses: adoration and agnosticism. Some worshiped him; some doubted his reality. By this time, all the doubts of the eleven, including those of the last holdout, Thomas, had been resolved.

How do you respond to the Lord Jesus Christ?

Do you worship?

Or do you doubt?

If you adore him, when is the last time you sank to your knees, prayed, and praised the living Lord with hymns of honor? At the close of Dr. Robert E. Coleman's doctoral class at Talbot Seminary this past summer, we men sank to our knees. The great commission ringing in our ears, tears flowed as we sang songs of praise and then prayed. I have ministered in the strength of that experience these past months.

> He is Lord, He is Lord.
> He is risen from the dead, and He is Lord.
> Every knee shall bow, every tongue confess,
> That Jesus Christ is Lord.

Try singing those lyrics sometime by yourself, in praise to God. I can hear the comments now. "Now Don, that's out of character for me. I'm too formal to get on my knees to sing and praise God." I can only say in reply that if that's the case, you'd better get used to it. As the book of Revelation describes it, there'll be a whole lot of kneeling and a whole lot of bowing and a whole lot of singing going on in heaven. Take a look at Revelation 5:8-9,10-14 and 7:11-17 if you don't believe me.

One group at Galilee greeted the Lord with adoration and praise. Another group did not. The agnostics, the doubters, still couldn't believe it. Maybe they'd heard rumors of a robbed tomb. Maybe they figured it was some kind of trick. No matter how convincing the evidence, they would not be persuaded.

It's the same today, and similar categories apply. We're in one camp, or the other. We believe, or we don't. There's no room and no time for neutrality. Putting off the decision really means saying no.

The Farewell Address. Facing this audience of adoring subjects and doubting skeptics, the Lord delivered a farewell address. He would be seen twice more before ascending, and he would also appear to Paul after his ascension, but this was the great commission, the unfolding of his plan for worldwide evangelism.

What were the final words Christ chose to leave with his assembled disciples and followers? In closing, the Lord made three points about his power, his plan, and his presence.

His Power. "All authority has been given to me in heaven and on earth," Jesus began (Matthew 28:18). Before going any further, he established his right to speak. All authority had been granted to him. Any authority in the world today has been delegated by the Lord Jesus. Think about it. How much the strong statements of the savior differ from his groans at Gethsemane. Then it was, "Father, if it is possible, let this cup pass from Me; yet not as I will, but as Thou wilt" (Matthew 26:39 NASB). Now, standing in his resurrected body, Jesus claimed all authority as his own. The sufferer is now sovereign; the victim is victor.

The Plan. The victor went on to reveal his plan. The Lord left a job description for each of those who worship him. If you're still a skeptic, this is not for you. If you're a believer, then you've been commissioned into his heavenly army. Pay attention, because you'll be graded up there on how well you handle the assignments down here. In his great commission, the Lord issued a threefold set of orders:

1. *"Go therefore and make disciples of all the nations."* We Christians have a responsibility to communicate the message of salvation to the world. We've got to tell others about Jesus

Christ. It's life over lip too. We've got to show the savior in our conduct as well as in our speech (see 1 Peter 3:15).

This evangelism ought to start with your own family. How sad it would be to lead thousands to Christ, but not your own son or daughter. Ingersoll's father was a preacher, remember.

Telling the news is a divine imperative. We can't take it or leave it. We are, as Paul says, "ambassadors for Christ" (see 2 Corinthians 5:20). We'd better not be too busy or too shy or too unsure of ourselves. We must commit our lifestyles to reflecting the savior. We've got to be ready to give an account of him to any who ask. We are commissioned to pass it on, share it with others. How refreshing it is to be around believers who long to share their faith. New Christians are often the most delightful; their gratitude to God bubbles over into a desire to tell their unsaved friends about Jesus.

2. *"Baptizing them in the name of the Father and the Son and the Holy Spirit."* Section two of the great commission points to the baptism of the believers we tell about Jesus. It means we encourage new Christians to mark their decisions for Christ. When the Ethiopian eunuch received Jesus as savior, he asked Philip to baptize him (see Acts 8:35ff). Baptism is a divine ordinance, like the Lord's supper. It is an act of obedience that identifies us with Christ Jesus. It is an expression of our faith.

3. *"Teaching them to observe all that I commanded you."* We are to make disciples, followers of Jesus, converts by faith to him. We are to follow up on these believers and encourage their baptisms. And then we shouldn't drop the ball and run on to the next ones. We are to teach them about the Lord and his word.

Making disciples—it's telling them about the salvation of Jesus Christ. It's also showing them what obedience to him means. It's training them in the disciplines of the faith: how to pray, how to study the Bible, encouraging them to memorize scripture, showing them ways to share their faith with others.

We're going to encounter folks in various stages of the process. Some we lead to Christ; some we baptize; some we disciple. Right now I am meeting with Les, my friend from Hide-A-Way mentioned earlier. We get together weekly for Bible study, discussion, scripture memorization, and prayer. I may be helping him some, but his insights amaze me. They're so refreshing, and I'm learning as much as he is.

You can become a believer and keep your mouth shut for the rest of your life, never telling anybody about Jesus Christ, and you'll still go to heaven. But you're not going to hear, "Well done, thou good and faithful servant," when you get there. Each of us will be accountable to answer these three questions as we enter eternity:

> How many disciples did you make?
> How many were baptized?
> How many did you teach?

Keeping score isn't important. Amassing numbers isn't the idea. God will show you the people you're to witness to and disciple. You've just got to be obedient, willing, and ready.

The Presence. Jesus Christ concluded his farewell address with a promise of his presence: "And lo, I am with you all the days, until the consummation of the age" (Matthew 28:20). He'll be with us through it all. He'll empower us to obey the orders he's left us with. Just look at these words of promise from scripture to remind yourself that this is so:

> So do not fear, for I am with you;
> do not be dismayed, for I am your God.
> I will strengthen you and help you;
> I will uphold you with my righteous right hand
> (Isaiah 41:10 NIV).

> The Lord replied, "My Presence will go with
> you, and I will give you rest" (Exodus 33:14 NIV).

> Keep your lives free from the love of money and be content with what you have, because God has said,
> "Never will I leave you;
> never will I forsake you" (Hebrews 13:5 NIV).

In the Pews on Easter Sunday

The next time you attend a church service on Easter Sunday, look at the people in the pews around you. I guarantee you're going to see two types amid the many: adorers and agnostics. The faces of many believers shine so that the living Christ is truly there to behold. If you're not one of them, or if you feel you've lost your first love and would like to find him again, why don't you talk to one of the shining faces? They'd love to help you discover the beauty of a meaningful relationship with the Lord.

Christianity is not intellectual suicide. Ultimately, belief must be based on Christ and his credentials. And his credentials, as I hope this book has begun to convince you, are more than adequate. I'd like to leave you with four factors about Christ to contemplate:

1. The impact of his life on history
2. The reality of lives transformed because of him
3. The hundreds of prophecies fulfilled in him
4. The witnessed truth of his resurrection

Can anyone seriously consider these four and not proclaim, "Truly, this was the Son of God"?

It seems so. It seems there will always be the O'Hairs and the Ingersolls. But for every response of agnosticism, it seems there is a response of adoration, sometimes a most unlikely one.

Years ago Robert Ingersoll challenged a man to investigate the life of Christ and to portray Jesus in a dramatic narrative as a hero, a man among men, but a man all the same. The friend, also an agnostic, accepted the challenge, musing that he'd always thought the life of Christ would make an interesting romance. But a funny thing happened. In the process of researching the life of Christ, the agnostic author came face to face with the greatest life ever lived. Things reached the point where he was compelled to cry, "Verily, this was the Son of God!" And thus General Lew Wallace penned *Ben-Hur*, a very different narrative from the one originally planned. Yet why shouldn't it have been? By the time the final chapter was written, Wallace had committed his life to Jesus Christ.

And Madalyn Murray O'Hair? While registering her son Bill for ninth grade in Baltimore, she overheard some students praying. That episode launched her attack on school prayer, and ended in a suit which lasted over two years and eventually reached the Supreme Court, where it was decided in favor of the ban. The mother may have gained national attention with the action, but her son suffered beatings and social ostracism because of the family's stand.

But in 1980, the world changed for William Murray. In that year he accepted Jesus Christ as his savior, and today devotes his time in evangelism for him. His mother? Murray prays that she will convert. "She's just another sixty-nine-year-old white-haired woman who needs Jesus," he said of her at a recent Christian rally (Wright 156).

And indeed she is.

The real issue is not whether Christianity makes sense; it does. It's not that Christianity is irrational; it's eminently rational. The real issue is, ***will you or won't you become a Christian?***

Is your lifestyle preventing you? You don't want to give up some of the things you do? You're afraid of being laughed at? Ostracized? Ridiculed? Criticized?

In the light of eternity, can you afford *not* to consider the meaning of Easter?

What else gives meaning to our world?

Just Because He Lives

Gloria and Bill Gaither are lyricists and composers of songs and hymns like "The King Is Coming," "There's Something about That Name," and "Let's Just Praise the Lord." One of their best-loved hymns, a song that especially reflects their own philosophy of life, is "Because He Lives." This beautiful song captures the importance of the "resurrection principle in the daily routines of life," as the Gaithers describe it. "Because He Lives" was voted the "Gospel Song of the Year for 1974" by both ASCAP and the Gospel Music Association. Bill Gaither recalls the circumstances surrounding its writing:

> We wrote "Because He Lives" after a period of time when we had had a kind of dry spell and hadn't written any songs for a while. . . . Also at the end of the 1960s, when our country was going through some great turmoil with the height of the drug culture and the whole "God Is Dead" theory which was running wild . . . and also at the peak of the Vietnam War, our little son was born—Benjy—at least Gloria was expecting him. And I can remember at the time we thought, "Brother, this is really a poor time to bring a child into the world." At times we were even quite discouraged by the whole thing. And then Benjy did come. We had two little girls whom we love very much, but this was our first son, and so that lyric came to us, "How sweet to hold our new-born baby and feel the pride and joy he gives, but better still the calm assurance that this child can face uncertain days because Christ lives." And it gave us the courage to say "Because Christ lives we can face tomorrow" and keep our heads high, and hopefully that could be of meaning to other people.

> It's rather interesting now that, although we don't consider ourselves "old" writers, we've had many people tell us they have used that song at a funeral of a loved one, and it has been very encouraging to them, at a time when they were very discouraged. So evidently a lot of people have shared the same kind of experience of being discouraged (Osbeck 286-287).

The resurrection? It gives meaning to our lives. In the words of Bill and Gloria Gaither, "And life is worth the living just because He lives." With the Gaithers' permission, I've reprinted the lyrics to the entire hymn below. Do your heart a favor, and sing it this season.

God sent His Son, they called him Jesus,
He came to love, heal, and forgive;
He lived and died to buy my pardon,
An empty grave is there to prove my Savior lives.

(Refrain)
Because He lives I can face tomorrow,
Because He lives all fear is gone;
Because I know He holds the future.
And life is worth the living just because He lives.

How sweet to hold a new-born baby,
And feel the pride, and joy he gives;
But greater still the calm assurance,
This child can face uncertain days because He lives.

And then one day I'll cross the river,
I'll fight life's final war with pain;
And then as death gives way to victory,
I'll see the lights of glory and I'll know He lives.

Reflections for the season

1. It is intellectually more difficult to discount the resurrection than to believe the evidence.

2. If we know Christ as savior, we're in the Lord's army. What three orders does Jesus instruct believers to accomplish in Matthew 28:19-20, the great commission? What are some ways you can start being about the Lord's business today?

3. When is the last time you sang praises to the Lord? Prayed to him spontaneously? Sank to your knees in thanksgiving? Met with another Christian friend and carried the conversation beyond sports or kids, the stock market or politics, actually to discussing the things of the Lord? No matter how long it has been, try it, soon.

CHAPTER NINE

The Resurrection

The annual Emerald Bay Easter egg hunt. You should be there! The event takes place each Easter at the home of my daughter and son-in-law, Donna and Mark Skorheim, after Sunday school and church. Consider this your invitation, but understand that there is an age limit set for participants. The eggs are hidden for church and neighborhood children and grandchildren, not for grownups longing to relive the experiences of Easters long ago.

Still, according to Mark and Donna, it is worth a trip to see how some of the grownups get into the act anyway. Two-and three-year-old boys and girls find a candy egg or two and are delighted by the discovery. Many young children soon give up the hunt and plop down to play with their treasures—if their parents and grandparents will let them, that is. Most of the time little Jimmy or Jill is dragged upright and coaxed and coached to resume the search. "Look! Do you see what I see?" exclaim proud parents, pointing at the "hidden" egg to which they've pulled their little participant. "Pick it up, honey! There's another one for your basket! I see a pink one near that tree! Looky there, next to the bush . . . get it, quick!" There's got to be a lesson in the fact that the small children are often satisfied with an egg or two, while the big folks are the ones who urge them on to greater grabbing.

Along with the hundreds of plastic candy-filled eggs and cellophane-wrapped marshmallow eggs that Mark and Donna conceal in their yard, several special eggs are also hidden. These contain slips of paper with numbers written on them, and the child lucky enough to find one is rewarded with a large chocolate Easter bunny as a prize. As you can imagine, the competition can be fierce.

One year, to pump up the enthusiasm of the children, Mark and Donna set out eight packaged chocolate rabbits on a table in the driveway where all the kids could ooh and ahh over them. Easter fell on a glorious sunny hot April day, and with unusual eagerness the children scrambled for the prize-winning special eggs. Notice I mentioned it was a *hot* April day. Five minutes after they'd set the chocolate rabbits out on the driveway and signaled the start of the hunt, Mark and Donna returned to fetch the prizes and put them inside. It was too late. The sunshine had done its work. Chocolate puddles were all that remained of each boxed bunny. A syrupy mess seeped from each plastic-coated cardboard package. Tiny candy eyes floating in the sweet sticky brown goo were all that remained to remind everyone that thirty dollars worth of chocolate rabbits, now prematurely deceased, had once awaited their fate at the grubby fingers and open mouths of hungry children.

Chocolate rabbits melting in the sun, Easter lilies wilting in the heat, colored eggs cracking as they're dropped—the symbols of Easter are terribly temporal, aren't they? They're eaten, planted (soon to die if planted in my yard), or discarded not long after Easter Sunday surrenders to Easter sunset.

I think it's good, therefore, to focus each Easter on what's essential instead of on what's extraneous. Let's be aware of what's temporary, and of what's eternal.

The essential? The eternal? What are they?

They're what the apostle Paul reminds us of in 1 Corinthians 15, and it's with a brief look at that passage that I'd like to leave you.

THE ESSENTIAL

Many folks ask me this question: Must I believe in the resurrection of Christ to be a Christian? You can lump that inquiry with others like:

Do I have to believe in the virgin birth of Christ to be a believer?

Must I accept the whole Bible in order to be a Christian?

The answer to all of these is yes. God said it; and if we want to know his Son as savior and Lord, we've got to believe it. That settles it.

Christianity is a package deal. We can't pick and choose which parts of the Bible we'll accept and which we'll reject. "All Scripture is inspired by God and profitable for teaching, for reproof, for correction, for training in righteousness," wrote Paul (2 Timothy 3:16 NASB). Notice, the verse says *all* scripture. We can't discount the divinity of Jesus, the inspiration and authority of scripture, the reality of the virgin birth and the resurrection, or any of the other portions of God's word, if we're going to claim to know Christ. Anything short of total acceptance equals unbelief, and that's a decision each of us must make individually.

To believe in the resurrection or not to believe in it? It's a choice some of the people at Corinth were confronting when the letter from Paul we call 1 Corinthians reached them. He was writing over twenty-five years after the crucifixion and resurrection. The members of the church in Corinth had become divided among themselves because they'd been following various teachers instead of the Christ and his message.

The believers to whom Paul wrote were quite carnal, and were childish in their faith. Some of them were doubting God's promise that Christians who had died would eventually be bodily resurrected. The Corinthians were also tolerating immorality in their ranks and were suing one another in courts of law. They were misusing spiritual gifts and some were even behaving improperly at the Lord's table, actually becoming drunk at communion. The church was in deep trouble, so Paul wrote to the Corinthian Christians with the intention of teaching them how God would have them deal with the divisiveness and the disobedience running rampant.

Had Christ arisen? That's the first question Paul answered in 1 Corinthians 15, reminding his readers that he had "delivered to you as of first importance what I also received, that Christ died for our sins according to the Scriptures, and that He was buried, and that He was raised on the third day according to the Scriptures" (15:2-3 NASB).

Yes, there had been a resurrection. Christ had arisen. Notice, Paul said that Christ's death, burial, *and resurrection* are of first importance. They are vital. They are absolutely essential. The resurrection is true beyond a shadow of a doubt. It is, as we've discussed previously, one of the best substantiated facts in scripture.

In this book, we've seen the resurrection records of Matthew, Mark, Luke, and John. We've observed the responses of those who loved Jesus. We've seen lives forever changed from encounters with him.

We must never forget that the risen Lord appeared to hundreds of eyewitnesses. Paul reminds us of this in verses 5 through 11 of 1 Corinthians 15. It wasn't just one fellow who came along and said, "I think I met Jesus." Then we'd have a right to say, "Go on—you're hallucinating, friend!" But with the six eyewitness experiences Paul mentioned, we'd have to cast aspersions on the characters of hundreds of people in order to destroy their testimonies. It just can't be done credibly.

Who had seen the Christ? Paul reminded us of Christ's appearances to Peter, to the disciples, to the five hundred, to James, and to himself. As we've discussed, Paul himself met the risen Lord on the road to Damascus (see Acts 9). This special appearance of Jesus occurred after his ascension (Acts 1:9) and changed Paul's heart and mind for all time, transforming him from a zealous persecutor of Christians to a man aflame for the Lord Jesus Christ. Before meeting Christ on the Damascus road, Paul (then known as Saul) stood watching the cloaks of those who stoned Stephen, the first martyr of the faith. He looked on in approval as rocks were hurled and Stephen's body was bruised and crushed (see Acts 7:58; 8:1).

But he changed after meeting Christ—from selfishness to selflessness, from cold-heartedness to caring, from self-righteousness to sympathy.

Yes, the Christ had risen. The documentation is extensive. Twenty-five years down the pike, as Paul wrote 1 Corinthians, the testimonies of eyewitnesses still rang true.

What If the Resurrection Isn't True?

Yes, there is a resurrection. Yet people still question its veracity. Some men and women in the Corinthian church evidently also did. "Now if Christ is preached, that He has been raised from the dead, how do some among you say that there is no resurrection of the dead?" (1 Corinthians 15:12 NASB). In other words, why is it that some of you still doubt? How can you possibly overlook the evidence?

You're too skeptical? Too sophisticated? You just can't bring yourself to admit that something you can't humanly explain might be true anyway? Maybe you accept the resurrection of Christ, but you don't believe that other believers will one day be raised as well? Paul was ready with answers to these questions too. Beginning with verse 13, he played a little intellectual game with his readers; so get ready. It's the *what if* game. Specifically the apostle asked: What if the resurrection weren't true?

Let's look at what Paul had to say.

1. *But if there is no resurrection of the dead, not even Christ has been raised* (1 Corinthians 15:13 NASB). No resurrection? That means Jesus is still in the grave. If that's true, do you know what that means? It means that Christianity is like every

other religion in the world. The bones of Jesus Christ are in a tomb somewhere, just like the remains of Confucius, Mohammed, or Buddha. We have no living leader. We're no different from any Muslim, Hindu, Buddhist, or Taoist. We have no lasting answers to the problems of humankind.

2. *And if Christ has not been raised, then our preaching is vain* (1 Corinthians 15:14 NASB). No resurrection? Then I'd better quit my job as a minister of the gospel. There's no sense in my preaching about an impotent God, is there? I'd only be talking about the history of a dead human leader. Why bother? Bible studies, Christian fellowship, worship hours, prayer meetings—all of them would be meaningless. They'd be like melted chocolate rabbits. They'd count for nothing.

3. *Your faith also is vain* (1 Corinthians 15:14 NASB). And what else is futile, if Christ hasn't been raised? Your faith, that's what. It's empty. You have no hope. You're just like the atheist Bertrand Russell, who described the life of man as "a long march through the night, surrounded by invisible foes, tortured by weariness and pain, towards a goal that few can hope to reach and where none can tarry long."

Do you want that eulogy read at your funeral? No thanks! But it's true if there's no resurrection. Then your faith, like my preaching, would be only sound and fury, signifying nothing.

4. *Moreover we are even found to be false witnesses of God, because we witnessed against God that He raised Christ, whom He did not raise, if in fact the dead are not raised. For if the dead are not raised, not even Christ has been raised* (1 Corinthians 15:15-16 NASB). Is Christ still dead? Then Paul is a liar. So are the disciples. So are the five hundred brethren. So is the Lord's own half-brother, James. With nothing to gain, they've perjured themselves. They've all borne false witness, for no legitimate reason. Why? It surely wasn't to get

ahead in the world, since the label *Christian* set them apart from the religious establishment and made the government suspicious of them, if not outright hostile toward them. The mere thought of lying made a man of honor like Paul shudder. A false witness? No, he was unflinchingly honest. It was against his character to lie, but a liar he'd be if there were no resurrection.

5. *And if Christ has not been raised, your faith is worthless; you are still in your sins* (1 Corinthians 15:17 NASB). If Christ hasn't been raised, your faith is worthless. That's not the same as being empty or meaningless, because worthlessness has consequences. It means you've missed the boat. You'd better start trying to be a better person, develop your personal karma, donate big bucks to charities, because you're still a sinner. You haven't been cleansed by the blood. A holy God will still condemn you. You're going to have to become perfect all by yourself. And you're never going to make it.

You're no murderer, you say? Good. But Jesus said that if you've ever even been angry with another, you've as good as killed him (Matthew 5:22). Our actions may not get us, but our thoughts will. Have you ever been selfish, even once? Have you envied a friend's promotion? Lost your temper? Yelled at your kids? Hollered at another driver on the freeway? Looked longingly at a member of the opposite sex other than your spouse? All it takes is one transgression, one misdeed, even one teeny tiny wrong thought, and you've missed the mark of God's holiness. You've sinned and fallen short of the glory of God, as Romans 3:23 puts it. You've failed to achieve the perfection of the Father and there's no hope of heaven for you—unless the resurrection is true.

6. *Then those also who have fallen asleep in Christ have perished* (1 Corinthians 15:18 NASB). You know what else is true if the resurrection isn't? Our loved ones who have pro-

fessed faith in Christ and died are simply dead. They're gone forever. We're never going to see them again. There's nothing beyond the grave. It means I'll not perform any more funerals, because I'll be able to point to nothing. Your deceased Christian brother or sister is kaput, eternally annihilated, vaporized into oblivion. There is not a shred of hope beyond the grave, if there is no resurrection.

7. *If we have hoped in Christ in this life only, we are of all men most to be pitied* (1 Corinthians 15:19 NASB). Finally, if there is no resurrection, our present lives are hopeless. We're deluded creatures. We've nothing to be excited about, no expectations of a future beyond this life. Jesus hasn't gone to prepare a place for us. It doesn't get any better than this, right now, today. We go around only once in life, so we'd better grab the brass ring while we can. Everything that is under the sun is *everything that is*, if there's no resurrection.

What if there's no resurrection? To sum it up, according to Paul, then Christ hasn't been raised. Our preaching amounts to nothing. Our faith is empty. People like Paul are liars. We're still dead in our sins. Deceased Christians have perished. Our present life is hopeless and pathetic.

But the resurrection is true. Christ is alive. We have eyewitness accounts. We have the *hard evidence* of an empty tomb, a discarded shroud, a divine messenger. We have the *heart evidence* of changed lives, of murderous hatred becoming intense love, of cowards becoming courageous, of the heartsick becoming encouraged. It is true!

8. *But now Christ has been raised from the dead* (1 Corinthians 15:20 NASB). The bleak picture is suddenly splashed with light. It's as if handfuls of glitter have been thrown on a coal-black canvas.

The central—and eternal—question is: What are you going to do with the truth that Jesus is alive?

The Calendar of Coming Events
Or, Since the Resurrection Is True, What's Next?

We live in an insane world, or so it seems. Israelis polish their guns on the Lebanese border. Syrians stockpile chemical weaponry for potential use against the Jewish state. The United States and the Soviet Union, despite Gorbachev and *glasnost* and *perestroika*, continue a nuclear arms race to which there can reasonably be no peaceful finish. The Persian Gulf stays a simmering volcano of potential conflict, ripe for a gigantic eruption superseding in horror even such incidents as the sinking of ships or the downing of military aircraft. Commercial airliners are blasted from the skies by missiles or concealed bombs, plummeting hundreds to fiery deaths. Chinese students die by the thousands at the hands of fellow countrymen in Beijing. A self-admitted terrorist addresses the United Nations. IRA "freedom fighters" plant bombs in shopping centers and public transports. Nuclear technology falls into the hands of maniacal Third World dictators. National economies collapse. The most powerful nation in the world is mortgaged to the tip of the capitol dome with a multi-billion-dollar deficit. Devastating, incurable diseases ravage whole segments of the most medically advanced countries in existence today. Children are snatched off our streets and disappear forever. Devil worshipers murder victims in cult rituals.

It is insane, isn't it?

Let's face it: life is crazy.

Now let's qualify that remark. Life is crazy, without Christ.

You see, God has a specific plan for the rest of time as we know it. He's already written the script, and handed it to us in his holy word. Beginning with 1 Corinthians 15:20, Paul referred to this unfolding panorama of world events as he threw off the shroud of *what ifs*, and uncovered the beauty of *what's to come*. Let's look at what he had to say.

> But now Christ has been raised from the dead, the first fruits of those who are asleep. For since by a man came death, by a man also came the resurrection of the dead. For as in Adam all die, so also in Christ all shall be made alive. But each in his own order: Christ the first fruits, after that those who are Christ's at His coming, then comes the end, when He delivers up the kingdom to the God and Father, when He has abolished all rule and all authority and power (1 Corinthians 15:20-24 NASB).

Take a good look at Paul's words. He brought up at least five facts affecting us all.

Fact number one. "Christ has been raised from the dead." Period. It has happened. Jesus reigns over death, over the grave, over our grief. What a joyous outburst in comparison to the dreary picture we've been contemplating. Peter said it too. "And God raised Him up again, putting an end to the agony of death, since it was impossible for Him to be held in its power" (Acts 2:24 NASB).

Fact number two. Christ is the "first fruits of those who are asleep." The offering of the first fruits is described in the Old Testament (Exodus 23:16; 34:26; Leviticus 2:12). The farmer would bring the first sheaves of grain and present them to the Lord as an offering of love. He would give to God the first-fruits of the harvest.

In experiencing bodily resurrection and ascension into heaven, Jesus Christ is the firstfruit of a vast harvest that will follow. It's the harvest of souls, a resurrection including everyone who comes to know Jesus as savior before experiencing physical death. Christ's resurrection guarantees the resurrection of every Christian. Because he lives, we shall live also.

Fact number three. We are born in "Adam," and must be reborn in Christ if we're to experience the resurrection. Paul explained in 1 Corinthians 15:21-22: "For since by a man came death, by a man also came the resurrection of the dead. For as in Adam all die, so also in Christ all shall be made alive" (NASB). Through the disobedience of one man, Adam, all humankind inherited a sin nature, a natural inclination to rebel against God. Every baby is born into this world in Adam, with that same sin nature. We are born in Adam, and will grow up spiritually dead, separated from God. We'll physically die that way too, if we are not first reborn by faith into the family of Jesus Christ.

"Enter by the narrow gate; for the gate is wide, and the way broad that leads to destruction, and many are those who enter by it," Jesus said (Matthew 7:13 NASB), referring to the choice that most persons will make. The broad way? It's the path of spiritual death, because the majority of the world's population through the ages has not, and will not, respond to Christ. Putting our lives on automatic pilot and doing nothing about our eternal destinies purchases us a one-way ticket to the fiery furnace.

A tract I saw the other day illustrates this. On the cover was a printed question: "What must I do to be lost?" Inside, the pages were blank. The tract was right on target. If we want to be lost for eternity—spiritually dead, permanently separated from God—then all we have to do is to do nothing.

Fact number four. The choice is yours. A decision must be made to step out of Adam and step into Christ. Those are the only two possibilities. There's no vast in-between region of indecision. If you're uncertain about whether you're in Adam or Christ, you're probably still in Adam. You know it when you know Jesus Christ. God's Spirit comes to dwell within you. He seals your brand-new relationship with the Son. You're a new creation.

There is no neutral ground. You're either the thief on the

cross who responds, or you're the thief who rejects. Those are the only two ways you can have it.

Fact number five. There is a definite order in which we'll experience resurrection. Who will be resurrected? Everyone! There will be two resurrections: the first, of the just; the second, of the unjust. The first resurrection will take place in three stages. Stage one happens at the resurrection of Christ—it's already been accomplished. It's history. Next, according to Paul, "Each in his own order; Christ the first fruits, after that those who are Christ's at His coming" (1 Corinthians 15:23 NASB). Stage two of this first resurrection will take place at the rapture, when we who belong to him shall be raised—first the dead Christians, then the living ones. We'll all be transformed, receiving shiny new bodies that will never wear out. Stage three will happen after the tribulation, and will involve those who become believers during that time of trial and are martyred, plus the Old Testament saints who will also then be raised (see Revelation 7:14; 20:4-6; Daniel 12:2; 1 Thessalonians 4:16-18; 1 Corinthians 15:51-54).

The exciting thing is that stage number two, the rapture of the church, could happen this very day, right now while you're reading this. Perhaps in the middle of this very night. Your head may hit the pillow at 11:00 p.m., and your feet may never again touch the floor. It thrills me to think of it!

I'm so grateful that I know God through Christ Jesus, and that my passage upward has been paid for. We're on standby, waiting for the final call.

What If I Never Accept the Resurrection?

As we've discussed, if you reject the resurrection, you're also rejecting the Christ who was raised from the dead. You're choosing to remain in Adam. I'm not trying to scare you, but if you make the choice to disbelieve, and you refuse to come to Jesus in faith, then I hope you've enjoyed your life on earth, because that's as good as it's going to get.

According to the Bible, you'll one day experience a resurrection too, the resurrection of the unjust. It's in only one stage, and it isn't pretty.. Revelation 20:11-15 describes the judgment you'll face at the great white throne. There you'll be judged according to your works, and you'll be condemned if you've failed to keep every single statute and ordinance of God's law. I'm not talking just about the ten commandments, but also about the over 630 regulations spelling out God's standards. If you've thought a wrong thought, even once, you'll not be holy enough to stand in the presence of a righteous God who cannot tolerate any shred of evil. Christ's blood sacrifice could have cleansed you of that unrighteousness, had you come to him in faith. But after you're dead, it'll be too late.

All who stand at the great white throne to be judged on the basis of their works will fail the test. They'll find that their names aren't written in the book of life. They'll be cast into the unimaginable agony of the lake of fire, there in torment to be eternally separated from God.

Consequences? Or Truth?

What can you do to avoid the great white throne? Deliberately, consciously, examine the claims of Jesus Christ. Consider your own life, and acknowledge that you have sinned and have fallen short of God's perfect standards. Accept Jesus Christ as the Son of God. Believe that he died to pay the penalty of your sins, and thereby receive him as savior. Acknowledge this decision as you talk with him in prayer.

What to do about Christ is the most crucial decision you will ever make. Will you come to him today? If your answer is yes, then talk to the Father and, in your own words, tell him these things:

1. Lord, I know that I am a sinner. I have missed the mark of your holiness. I have fallen short of your righteousness. I acknowledge the truth of Romans 3:23,

"For all have sinned and fall short of the glory of God" (NASB), and I know that it applies to me.

2. Lord, I believe that Jesus Christ died on the cross to pay the penalty for my sin. As Romans 5:8 says, "But God demonstrates His own love toward us, in that while we were yet sinners, Christ died for us" (NASB). Ephesians 2:8-9 says that salvation is a gift from you, by your grace, not something I could earn through human works or performance. I know that nothing I could ever do on my own would be worthy enough to merit your favor and forgiveness. *I am trusting Christ alone as my savior.*

3. Lord, thank you for coming into my life and making me your child.

Step three is simply an affirmation of your decision. It's also good to record the decision somewhere permanently, for future assurance. Perhaps you'll want to do so in your Bible, or even in the blanks below:

I, ____________________, received Jesus Christ as savior on ____________ (day), ____________ (month), ____________ (year), ____________ (time). Signed, ____________________.

Many people do not remember a specific moment of trusting Christ or praying to him. They agonize and worry. I ask them, "Whom are you trusting now?" If they say, "Jesus," I say, "Okay! You've nothing to worry about." A prayer does not save us. It marks our decision. Trusting Jesus Christ saves us. That's it. That's all. Once you make the decision to trust Christ, you are in the family of God forever. Once reborn, you'll never be unborn either. Your salvation is secure. As Jesus said, "My sheep hear My voice, and I know them, and they follow Me; and I give eternal life to them, and they shall never perish; and no one shall ever snatch them out of My hand" (John 10:27-28 NASB; see also 10:29).

What's next? It's time to grab hold of your Bible and learn more about the Lord you've just come into relationship with. The gospel of John is a good place to begin reading. And here are some verses from various sections of scripture to get you going: 1 John 5:11-12; John 16:24; 1 Corinthians 10:13; 1 John 1:9; Proverbs 3:5-6.

It's also important to find a Bible-teaching, Bible-believing church in which to worship and fellowship. Seek out a mature Christian who is willing to disciple you; that is, to meet with you regularly and to answer your questions, to share insights into scripture, and to help you start on a program of study and memorization. If there is a conservative, evangelical organization such as Bible Study Fellowship in your area, attend it too. Digging into God's word and associating with other maturing believers are critical ingredients of growth.

Keeping the Flames Lit till the End

After Paul described the resurrection of Jesus, and that of all believers, he said, "Then comes the end, when He delivers up the kingdom to the God and Father, when He has abolished all rule and all authority and power" (1 Corinthians 15:24).

Scholars differ on the meaning of this verse, but I am convinced that it refers to the end of all time as we know it. At some point after a thousand-year reign, and after the great white throne judgment, Jesus Christ will deliver his kingdom to the Father. A new heaven and a new earth will be created. These events are described in Revelation 21 and 22, and also in 2 Peter 3:10-13. It's going to be wonderful! Imagine it—eternity alongside the Father in a spotless, sinless, re-created paradise. The death benefits to us believers boggle the mind, don't they? I don't know about you, but just thinking about *what will be* makes me ready for the ride up.

I can almost forget the present.

But as believers we can't afford the luxury of forgetting the present. A lost world awaits the news that we already know. We've been left on the planet for the purpose of conveying the message of Jesus Christ and his kingdom. We've much to do, in the meantime.

So, in the meantime, what do we do?

Easter is on its way. The season can be a goldmine for spreading the gospel. We're called to keep Christ at the helm of our hearts.

How can we keep Christ paramount this Easter? What methods can we use to remind ourselves that the season is more than a celebration of spring, a barrage of bunnies, a collection of candy eggs, bonnets, and baskets? How can we keep the truth of the risen Lord from being entombed underneath mountains of cellophane grass and boxed gift Bibles? What are some ways that the flames of our hearts can be rekindled for him? The hearts of others enkindled for him?

I have a few suggestions. Some will work for you and your situation. Some won't. Perhaps some will serve only to spark another idea in your mind. What's critical is that Christ not be forgotten as Easter envelops us. After all, he is the reason for the season.

Focusing on Christ This Easter

1. If you don't regularly attend church, Easter is a prime occasion for reversing that trend. It's time to change your habits. Determine to leave the holly-and-lily crowd and become part of a local congregation. Find a fellowship where you feel comfortable, but make sure that the teaching is Bible-based and conservative. Search for a church where scripture is accepted and taught literally. If these suggestions sound unclear, find a place where the preacher regularly takes a section of the Bible and explains it on Sunday mornings.

2. Have you been a believer for a while? Are you packed with

biblical knowledge? Are you maybe even getting a bit irritated because you feel you aren't being fed at your church or in your Bible studies? Are you searching for more spiritual depth? It's possible that you're a stuffed sheep ready to become a shepherd.

Instead of seeking sources of greater knowledge, this Easter start looking around for a new believer, someone who hasn't read as many commentaries or attended as many Bible classes as you. Get together with your new friend on a regular basis to go over a section of the word. Share insights. Memorize scripture. With your knowledge, you'll be able to clarify things for your friend, but I guarantee you'll be surprised at what you'll learn too. You're going to be blessed. It's only been recently, after thirty-plus years in ministry, that I've discovered the excitement and joy of one-on-one discipling. Don't wait as long as I did to find out what you're missing.

3. Do you feel that you don't know much about the Bible? Then this Easter, begin to search for someone like the person in number two above, who will meet with you on a regular basis. Start getting together weekly for study and sharing, perhaps over lunch or breakfast. You won't regret it.

4. As the familiar symbols of Easter begin to fill store shelves, take a new look at these traditional signs of the season. It's possible to bring the subject of Christ into conversations with your children, wife, husband, or friends while referring to even the most commonplace images of Easter. Here are a few suggestions:

a. *Easter eggs.* Originally pagan symbols, eggs suggest new life. And of course, on receiving Christ, we also receive a new life in him. Make the comparison.

b. *Lambs.* Stores stock almost as many of these stuffed critters as they do rabbits during the Easter season. Point at one sometime and take the opportunity to remind your friends and family that Jesus was the sacrificial lamb who came to take away the sin of the world. This works well with grandchildren, especially if you fork over a few dollars for a toy lamb they can take home.

c. *Easter lilies.* Take note of their trumpet-shaped heads. They herald the good news: Jesus Christ is risen! They are living object lessons of the message of salvation.

5. As a family, hold an Easter egg hunt for neighborhood children. Make sure there are plenty of colored eggs and candy for everyone, but also make this party into an "egg-stra" special event with a twist. At some point in the festivities, include a brief presentation of the gospel, explaining why we celebrate Easter in the first place. It can be a golden opportunity to share the good news. Jack and Jody Green, Child Evangelism Fellowship missionaries in San Antonio, Texas, put on such a shindig annually, inviting over eighty children to participate. Each year some of the guests find the savior. (Hint: gather everyone together for the Bible story *before* you turn them loose to hunt.)

6. Don't let yourself become entangled in excessive gift-giving this Easter. If you must give a gift, why not make it something to do with the Lord? A Bible, perhaps, or a devotional book or some inspirational Christian work would be good. Read something like that yourself too.

7. Approach the Easter season with a heart of gratitude to God for all he has done. Say thank you to him in an extra special way. Perhaps you could help some needy missionaries with additional financial support. Maybe you could take a trip to a nursing home and read scripture to an elderly person who can no longer do so.

Say thank you to the people-gifts God has given you too—namely, your family and special friends. You might make "We Love You Because" cards for each member of the family. Simply fold a piece of construction paper in two and on the outside print, "We Love Dad Because" or "We Love Mom Because" or "We Love Henry Because" and then allow others to complete the message inside in their own words. Our family did this recently, and the precious sentiments expressed are going to carry us all through the next year. When we start feeling low, we'll just look inside for instant encouragement.

8. This Easter, ask God to help you convey the truth of his greatest gift. Memorize verses to explain God's plan of salvation to others, and to lead them to Christ. Pray for God to give you opportunities to tell somebody else about him. Eventually there will be an open door. Your chance may not come as soon as you expect; it probably won't be when and where you anticipate either. It may be that the results won't be what you'd like. But your opportunity to communicate the kingdom will come. Be ready.

To Leave You With

The older I get, the more people I love are leaving this life. Since beginning work on this book, I've preached at twenty funerals of dear Christian brothers and sisters who've gone home to be with the Lord. Cancer has claimed them; traffic accidents have snatched them; cardiac diseases have silenced them. In this same period of time, televised newscasts have blared a litany of human tragedy and paraded visual evidence of the death that inevitably enshrouds our species. There is cold comfort in knowing that an unbeliever has perished. But how different are the funerals of the faithful.

The first Easter after you experience the loss of a special Christian friend or family member, never will the scripture seem more relevant, the promise of the resurrection more vivid, the hope of eventual heavenly reunion more real, the hymns more meaningful. Even the familiar hymn, "Low in the grave He lay—Jesus my Savior! Waiting the coming day—

Jesus my Lord! Up from the grave He arose," takes on fresh significance as our hearts long to see lost loved ones again. I know how I felt on that first Easter after preaching at the funeral of my dad. Friends who've recently surrendered parents, spouses, and children to the grave confirm that this is so. With each stanza of "Christ the Lord Has Risen Today," the words of Martha echo in our hearts and minds. Speaking of her just-deceased brother Lazarus, she said, "I know that he will rise again in the resurrection on the last day" (John 11:24 NASB).

"Lazarus, come forth," Jesus Christ commanded, minutes after his talk with Martha, and Lazarus did come forth (John 11:43-44), a tangible preview of coming attractions. The same Jesus whom the Father empowered to raise Lazarus has promised our resurrection as well.

"I am the resurrection and the life; he who believes in Me shall live even if he dies, and everyone who lives and believes in Me shall never die. Do you believe this?" the Lord asked of Martha (John 11:25-26).

It's a question he asks each of us too.

This Easter, may we not forget the ramifications of the resurrection.

Like Martha, may our answer be: "Yes, Lord; I have believed that You are the Christ, the Son of God, even He who comes into the world" (John 11:27 NASB).

Being involved in camps and conferences over the years, I have vivid memories of decision times around the communion table. Tears and testimonies, conversions and commitments, prayers and praises. We always end the times late into the night, joining hands in a big circle and singing Alfred H. Ackley's old favorite, "He Lives."

I serve a risen Savior,
He's in the world today;
I know that He is living,
Whatever men may say;

I see His hand of mercy,
I hear His voice of cheer,
And just the time I need Him,
He's always near.

Rejoice, rejoice, O Christian,
Lift up your voice and sing
Eternal hallelujahs
To Jesus Christ the King!
The Hope of all who seek Him,
The Help of all who find,
None other is so loving,
So good and kind.

He lives, He lives,
Christ Jesus lives today!
He walks with me and talks with me
Along life's narrow way.
He lives, He lives,
Salvation to impart!
You ask me how I know He lives?
He lives within my heart.

Amen. Come, Lord Jesus.

BIBLIOGRAPHY

About the cross and the resurrection:

Austin, E. L. C. 1979. *Earth's Greatest Day.* Grand Rapids, MI: Baker Book House.

Barclay, William. 1961. *Crucified and Crowned.* London: SCM Press, Ltd.

Barnhouse, Donald Grey. 1961. *The Cross through the Open Tomb.* Grand Rapids, MI: Wm. B. Eerdmans Publishing Company.

Dinsmore, Maret H. 1979. *What Really Happened When Christ Died.* Denver, CO: Accent Books.

Evans, W. Glyn, ed. 1977. *Christ is Victor.* Valley Forge, PA: Judson Press.

Gutzke, Manford G. 1974. *Plain Talk on the Resurrection.* Grand Rapids, MI: Baker Book House.

Huegel, F. J. 1949. *Calvary's Wondrous Cross.* Grand Rapids, MI: Zondervan Publishing House.

Jones, Russell Bradley. 1945. *Gold from Golgotha.* Chicago, IL: Moody Press.

Kuyper, Abraham. 1960. *The Death and Resurrection of Christ.* Grand Rapids, MI: Zondervan Publishing House.

Little, Paul E. 1967. *Know Why You Believe.* Wheaton, IL: Victor Books.

Lucado, Max. 1986. *No Wonder They Call Him the Savior: Chronicles of the Cross.* Portland, OR: Multnomah Press.

Maclaren, Alexander, Charles H. Spurgeon, D. L. Moody, T. DeWitt Talmage, and Canon Liddon. *Great Sermons on the Resurrection.* 1963. Grand Rapids, MI: Baker Book House. First published in 1896 by Fleming H. Revell under the title *Resurrection.*

MacArthur, John, Jr. 1975. *Can a Man Live Again?* Chicago, IL: Moody Press.

Marsh, F. E. n.d. *Why Did Christ Die?* Grand Rapids, MI: Zondervan Publishing House.

McDowell, Josh, comp. 1972. *Evidence That Demands a Verdict.* San Bernardino, CA: Campus Crusade for Christ International.

McGee, J. Vernon. n.d. *Christ, His Cross, and His Church.* Los

Angeles, CA: Church of the Open Door.
_____. 1968. *The Empty Tomb.* Glendale, CA: Gospel Light Publications.
Merton, Thomas. 1975. *He Is Risen.* Niles, IL: Argus Communications.
Meyer, F. B. 1959. *Calvary to Pentecost.* Grand Rapids, MI: Baker Book House.
Nicholson, William R. 1928. *The Six Miracles of Calvary.* Chicago, IL: Moody Press.
Pink, Arthur W. 1962. *The Seven Sayings of the Saviour on the Cross.* Grand Rapids, MI: Baker Book House.
Spurgeon, Charles Haddon. 1961. *Christ's Words from the Cross.* Grand Rapids, MI: Zondervan Publishing House.
Stalker, James M. 1961. *The Trial and Death of Jesus Christ.* Grand Rapids, MI: Zondervan Publishing House.
Thatcher, Floyd W., ed. and comp. 1972. *The Splendor of Easter.* Waco, TX: Word Books.

About the gospels and the life of Christ:

Barclay, William. 1955. *The Daily Study Bible: The Gospel of John.* 2 vols. Edinburgh: The Saint Andrew Press.
_____. 1953. *The Daily Study Bible: The Gospel of Luke.* Edinburgh: The Saint Andrew Press.
_____. 1954. *The Daily Study Bible: The Gospel of Mark.* Edinburgh: The Saint Andrew Press.
_____. 1957. *The Daily Study Bible: The Gospel of Matthew.* 2 vols. Edinburgh: The Saint Andrew Press.
Boice, James Montgomery. 1978. *The Gospel of John.* 5 vols. Grand Rapids, MI: Zondervan Publishing House.
Davies, Benjamin, ed. 1976. *Davies' Harmony of the Gospels.* Grand Rapids, MI: Baker Book House.
Edersheim, Alfred. 1956. *The Life and Times of Jesus the Messiah.* 2 vols. Grand Rapids, MI: Wm. B. Eerdmans Company.
Hendriksen, William. 1978. *New Testament Commentary The Gospel of Luke.* Grand Rapids, MI: Baker Book House.
_____. 1973. *New Testament Commentary: The Gospel of Matthew.* Grand Rapids, MI: Baker Book House.
Ironside, H. A. 1947. *Addresses on the Gospel of Luke.* Neptune,

NJ: Loizeaux Brothers, Inc.

———. 1948. *Expository Notes on the Gospel of Mark.* Neptune, NJ: Loizeaux Brothers, Inc.

———. 1948. *Expository Notes on the Gospel of Matthew.* Neptune, NJ: Loizeaux Brothers, Inc.

———. 1942. *Addresses on the Gospel of John.* Neptune, NJ: Loizeaux Brothers, Inc.

Keller, W. Phillip. 1977. *Rabboni.* Old Tappan, NJ: Fleming H. Revell.

Lucado, Max. 1987. *God Came Near: Chronicles of the Christ.* Portland, OR: Multnomah Press.

McGee, J. Vernon. 1983. *Thru the Bible with J. Vernon McGee.* Vol. 4, *Matthew-Romans.* Nashville, TN: Thomas Nelson Publishers.

Pentecost, J. Dwight. 1981. *The Words and Works of Jesus Christ.* Grand Rapids, MI: Zondervan Publishing House.

Scroggie, W. Graham. 1948. *A Guide to the Gospels.* London: Pickering and Inglis, Ltd.

Stott, John R. W. 1986. *The Cross of Christ.* Downers Grove, IL: InterVarsity Press.

Walvoord, John F. and Roy B. Zuck, eds. 1983. *The Bible Knowledge Commentary.* New Testament edition. Wheaton, IL: Victor Books.

Walvoord, John F. 1974. *Matthew: Thy Kingdom Come.* Chicago, IL: Moody Press.

Westcott, Brooke Foss. 1954. *The Gospel According to St. John.* Grand Rapids, MI: Wm. B. Eerdmans Publishing Company.

Wiersbe, Warren W. 1980. *Meet Your King.* Wheaton, IL: Victor Books.

ACKNOWLEDGMENTS

Brown, Joan Winmill. 1979. *Corrie: The Lives She's Touched.* Special edition published for World Wide Pictures by special arrangement with Fleming H. Revell Company. Minneapolis, MN: World Wide Pictures.

Collins, Monica. 1988. "Talking with Cos." *Ladies Home Journal* (January)105:113, 141.

Davis, Ron Lee. 1984. *A Forgiving God in an Unforgiving World.* Eugene, OR: Harvest House Publishers.

McDowell, Josh, comp. 1972. *Evidence That Demands a Verdict.* San Bernardino, CA: Campus Crusade for Christ International.

Osbeck, Kenneth W. 1985. *101 More Hymn Stories.* Grand Rapids, MI: Kregel Publications.

Roberts, Patti, and Sherry Andrews. 1983. *Ashes to Gold.* Waco, TX: Word Books.

Sandin, Fran Caffey. 1988. *See You Later Jeffrey.* Wheaton, IL: Tyndale House Publishers, Inc.

Whiston, William, trans. 1978. *Josephus: Complete Works.* Grand Rapids, MI: Kregel Publications.

Wright, Lawrence. 1989. "God Help Her." *Texas Monthly* 17(January):102-105, 153-158.

Popular pastor, teacher, and speaker Don Anderson tours Texas and neighboring states giving Bible classes and business luncheon seminars during the fall, winter, and spring months. During the spring and summer, Don Anderson Ministries sponsors numerous conferences, and youth and family camps. Don also preaches regularly at two churches staffed by the Ministries and speaks at Bible conferences in various locations in the United States and Canada. His audiences of business and professional men and women, housewives and tradespeople, testify that his refreshing teaching makes the scriptures "come alive" for them.

Don Anderson graduated from Northwestern College in 1955 with the bachelor of arts degree. He received the master of theology from Dallas Theological Seminary in 1959, and is currently completing work on a doctorate from Talbot Seminary. Don has been in Christian ministry for more than thirty years, serving as a Young Life staff member, youth pastor, program director at The Firs Bible and Missionary Conference, executive director of Pine Cove Conference Center, and, since 1972, as director of the nonprofit organization, Don Anderson Ministries, headquartered in Tyler, Texas.

Don Anderson has many audio and video cassette tapes based on his classes that are produced by the Ministries and distributed widely. There is also a Ministries newsletter, *The Grapevine*, which reaches about nine thousand homes.

If you would like to receive more information about the classes, camps, and conferences offered by the Ministries, or would like a free catalog of media resources available, please phone 214-597-3018 or write to this address:

Don Anderson Ministries
P.O. Box 6611
Tyler, Texas 75711